NOTES ON THE

INSTITUTION OF

PUNISHMENT

and CORRECTIONS

MONICA SOLINAS SAUNDERS

www.kendallhunt.com
Send all inquiries to:
4050 Westmark Drive
Dubuque, IA 52004-1840

Table of Content

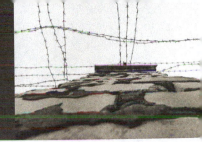

Section I

History of Punishment

Symbolic religious portrait of engraved persecuted Jesus who died torturously as a martyr or sufferer for biblical divine faith. The picture also showing followed disciples crying to torturer.

CHAPTER 1

Evolution of Punishment

Medieval Torture Equipment

LEARNING OBJECTIVES

- Identify significant changes in the administration of punishment over time
- Specify major milestones in the history of punishment
- Articulate main ideological shifts in the idea of punishment

INTRODUCTION

Punishment is as old as human kind. While a record of the first formal punishment against an accused does not exist, scientists agree that punishment rituals were routinely applied in the ancient world (Newman, 1985; Stearns, 1936). In primitive societies, punishment was applied as a reaction of "annoyance or irritation" toward those who did not conform to the desired conduct of the mainstream group (Stearns, 1936: 219). Punishment rituals always found expression in the response to sentiments of guilt and the institution of obedience. Religious practices appear to have shaped punishment in most social orders (Newman, 1985).

Evidence exists that punishment was formalized into criminal law in ancient civilizations (Newman, 1985). Similarities existed among criminal laws of Egyptians, Babylonians, Hindus, and Chinese civilizations. The most commonly cited body of law providing instructions for punishment is the Mosaic Law. The central principle of Mosaic Law, *lex talionis*, imposed that the accused be punished through a pain comparable to the one he inflicted to his victim. This retaliatory approach to punishment was also known as "*an eye for an eye*" (Newman, 1985).

Ancient forms of punishment were clear expression of vengeance meant to revenge the harm caused to the victim or the victim's family (Stearns, 1936). Despite the advancements in civil law practices during both the Greek and the Roman empires, criminal law remained at its primitive state in both societies. The Twelve Tables of Rome identified the head of the household (*pater familia*) as the one responsible to punish both his family members and his slaves (Newman, 1985). Slavery was also a form of punishment in Roman society, often used to punish debtors (Burdon, 1988).

Barbaric forms of punishment continued through the dark ages of feudal societies. During the Medieval Period, however, punishment rituals became justified by religious beliefs that reshaped the moral convictions. Stoning, beheading, mutilation, crucifixion, burning, and drowning were all used throughout the Middle-Ages in Europe (Newman, 1985). Punishment was chosen not only depending on the offense, but also depending on the offender's position in the social hierarchy (Newman, 1985).

An analysis of punishment across history reveals that societies have always used collective punishment as an attempt to reinstate the social order that an offense has the power to disrupt. Within this concept, the use of public forms of punishment, *the spectacle of the scaffold* become widely justified (Foucault, 1977). The description of the Damien's quartering after the regicide that occurred in France in 1757 is a reminder that torture continued to be the main form of punishment in Europe for a very long time (Foucault, 1977: 3).

According to Newman (1985: 7–11), throughout history, punishment has been defined on the basis of five principles:

- It must be unpleasant (or "normally considered" unpleasant).
- There must be a violation of a rule.
- It must be determined for an actual or supposed offender.
- It must be inflicted by others against an offender.
- It must be implemented by the same legal system that designed it.

While punishment and the field of penology have changed in many ways throughout the history of humanity, these principles still rule most modern systems of punishment.

THE INFLUENCE OF THE ENLIGHTENMENT

The most remarkable changes in the history of punishment can be explained within the advancements of the scientific revolution that occurred in Europe during the 17th century. "Reason" rather than "religious beliefs" became the established form of knowledge during the era of the *Enlightenment* (Foucault, 1977). The divorce from religious beliefs also led to the revolt against the oppression of the ruling classes. Examples of this were the French Revolution in Europe (1789–1790) and the American Revolutionary War (1775–1783). As human values were reshaped by the power of knowledge, *Natural Law* (with Montesquieu, Locke, and Rosseau) became the most accepted theory in Europe and contributed to the development of philosophies of punishment that characterized much of the Western ideologies throughout the 18th century and still influence Western institutions of punishment today (Newman, 1985). *Natural Law* became established for its ability to explain a universal moral code based on reason (Hart, 1958).

Several factors have contributed to the expansion of punishment throughout history, both in Europe and in the United States, as direct consequence of urbanism and population growth (De Long & Shleifer, 1993). The growth of the urban populations in Europe between the 13th and 19th centuries was often accompanied by the expansion of governments and the need to regulate poverty, idle, and vagrancy (Oliver & Hilgenberg, 2010). Lack of employment and local governments' inability to feed the poor led cities like Paris and London to adopt stricter forms of punishment to deal with the problem of "idle" (riots, fights, violence, prostitution, and theft) in the streets. In England, the chaos in the streets led to an expansion of the list of crimes punishable by death, with over 200 crimes punishable with the death penalty in the early 1700s (Oliver & Hilgenberg, 2010).

In 1718, with an act of Parliament, England began to transport convicts to the colonies, although cases of convict transportation had occurred much earlier since the early 1600s (Smith, 1934). Convicts eligible for transportation varied by matter of offense. Although some convicts were transported after committing a minor offense, many were accused of serious violent crimes (Smith, 1934). By the mid-1800s, torture had disappeared from most western European countries and quickly punishment became a hidden component of the entire penal process. On March 9, 1787, in Philadelphia, physician and social reformer Benjamin Rush, in an address to the Society for Promoting Political Enquiries, spoke openly against torture and promoted the idea of making punishment a nonpublic event (Foucault, 1977).

THE SHIFT FROM THE BODY TO THE SOUL

The almost complete abandonment of the use of torture as the main form of punishment meant that the body was no longer subjected to physical pain but it was "caught up in a system of constraints and privations, obligations, and prohibitions" (Foucault, 1977: 11). Within this new philosophy of punishment, inflicting pain to the offender became difficult to manage. A certain distance between the executioner and the executed was necessary. In England, for instance, the use of the hanging machine was introduced in the 1760s and later perfected in

1783. In France, the guillotine was first used in 1792, transforming death by punishment into an "instantaneous event" (Foucault, 1977: 13).

Some may argue that the conscious attempt to reduce physical pain in punishment allowed focusing on the "soul" rather than the body, making punishment a more insidious form of social control that would affect the deepest part of one's human experience, the mind. As Foucault put it, "[t]he soul is the effect and instrument of a political anatomy; the soul is the prison of the body" (Foucault, 1977: 30). As the physical flagellation of the body disappeared from the political discourse on punishment, the politics of punishment emerged as a major discipline both in Europe and the United States. This shift appears to have allowed punishment to embody a complex and important social function.

As punishment became institutionalized within a system that uses confinement in jails, prisons, and detention centers as the main measures of public safety, the offender's deprivation of personal liberties replaced the use of corporal punishment.

THE CONNECTION BETWEEN PUNISHMENT AND THE ECONOMY

Foucault (1977) discussed punishment as an important element of political economy. While physical deprivation might make sense within economic systems that use slavery as a primary form of labor and social control, capitalism needs free and able bodies of production in a free market. Capitalism and the penal system are intertwined within this perspective. Historians and criminologists have attempted to explain punishment and the penal system as an instrument of capitalism in several instances in modern literature (Alexander, 2012; Davis, 2003). The use of jails, prisons, and detention centers in today's penal systems is an example of how a huge punishment apparatus can feed the economy by creating new opportunities for corporate builders and service providers while at the same time positively influencing employment rates by providing jobs to low skilled individuals (Alexander, 2012). In addition, by isolating the most marginalized, the institutionalization of offenders contributes to the exclusion of certain groups from active participation in the labor market, even allowing for a recalculation of unemployment rates as thousands of unemployed individuals (often unemployable) are kept behind bars (Petersilia, 2003).

LEARNING EXERCISES

- Create a timeline of major changes that occurred in the use of punishment throughout history.
- Discuss the influence of the Enlightenment (or the era of reason) on the changes that occurred in the field of penology.
- Write your reflections on the idea that punishment has shifted from the body to the soul.
- Discuss in what ways punishment has become an instrument of capitalism in modern societies. Do you agree with this idea? Why?

BIBLIOGRAPHY

Alexander, M. (2012). *The new Jim Crow: Mass incarceration in the age of colorblindness*. New York, NY: The New Press.

Burdon, J. (1988). Slavery as a punishment in Roman criminal law. In L. J. Archer (Ed.), *Slavery and other forms of unfree labour* (pp. 68–85), New York, NY: Routledge.

Davis, A. Y. (2003). Race and criminalization: Black Americans and the punishment industry. In E. McLaughlin & J. Muncie (Eds.), *Criminological perspectives: Essential readings* (2nd ed., pp. 284–293), London, UK: Sage Publications Ltd.

De Long, J. B., & Shleifer, A. (1993). Princes and merchants: European city growth before the industrial revolution. *The Journal of Law and Economics*, *36*(2), 671–702.

Foucault, M. (1977). *Discipline and punish: The birth of the prison*. Trans. Sheridan A. London: Penguin Books.

Hart, H. L. A. (1958). Positivism and the separation of law and morals. *Harvard Law Review*, *71*(4), 593–629.

Newman, G. R. (1985). *The punishment response*. Albany, NY: Transaction publishers.

Oliver, W. M., & Hilgenberg, J. F. (2010). *A history of crime and criminal justice in America*. Durham, NC: Carolina Academic Press.

Petersilia, J. (2003). *When prisoners come home: Parole and prisoner reentry*. New York, NY: Oxford University Press.

Smith, A. E. (1934). The transportation of convicts to the American colonies in the seventeenth century. *The American Historical Review*, *39*(2), 232–249.

Stearns, A. W. (1936). The evolution of punishment. *Journal of Criminal Law and Criminology (1931–1951)*. *27*(2), 219–230.

CHAPTER 2

Philosophies of Punishment Influencing Corrections

Jeremy Bentham (1748–1832). Engraved by J. Pofselwhite and published in The Gallery of Portraits With Memoirs encyclopedia, United Kingdom, 1833.

LEARNING OBJECTIVES

- Define the philosophies of punishment that dominated both the European and American political discourse throughout the 18th century

- Identify the differences among the various philosophies of punishment of the 18th and 19th centuries

- Articulate the characteristics of Positivism in in penology and its influence on modern ideas of criminality

INTRODUCTION

The reaffirmation of reason as the pillar of social organization created a philosophical shift in theories of punishment. The question "when (morally) ought we to punish?" governed the institution of punishment throughout the Middle Ages. As reason became an essential element in the design of social arrangements, a new question had to be addressed in the analysis of punishment: "when (logically) should we punish?" (Clarke, 1982). The underlying difference between these two philosophical inquiries lies on the idea that, while a moral focus on punishment stems from religious beliefs (not necessarily upheld by all members of society), a logical focus on punishment implies that guilt is the essential element in the determination of punishment. With reason entering the realm of penology, a major change occurred in the way crime, punishment, and the offender were perceived.

THE CLASSIC DEBATE ON PUNISHMENT

A relevant contribution to the classic debate on punishment came from Cesare Beccaria, an Italian intellectual who influenced the development of philosophies of punishment both in Europe (especially in Italy and England) and in the United States. Beccaria's book "Dei Delitti e delle pene" (On Crime and Punishment), published in 1764, is still considered an important pillar of our system of punishment (Draper, 2000). Harcourt defined Beccaria's "On Crime and Punishment" as "a manifesto for legal reform centered on the Enlightenment values of rationality, proportionality, legality, lenience, and the rule of law" (2013: 1). Beccaria gained popularity especially because he rejected cruelty and barbarism that were still used to punish offenders during his time. Influenced by Natural Law theories that put human life and human rights at the center of social organization, Beccaria focused on contractual egalitarianism to explain crime as a function of both individual and social determinants to develop a new perspective on crime and punishment. Beccaria's perception of social interactions was that people are in perpetual conflict, as one's personal interest tends to prevail over that of society. Per Beccaria, the law provides the necessary contract to maintain social order (Beccaria, 1764) and punishment is used to avoid that individuals continuously throw society into chaos.

Beccaria believed that punishment ought to be proportionate to the offense and applied with certainty and immediacy. He argued that those who break the law should not lose their rights; the offender is also deserving of respect in the moment punishment is applied. This is an important principle of Beccaria's ideology, often omitted within classical and contemporary interpretations of his work (Draper, 2000). Judicial tortures and the death penalty did not find justification in Beccaria' contractual explanation of punishment. For the law to be effective within a secular judicial system, Beccaria explained, punishment must protect the innate value of human life. The death penalty represented a true failure of the penal system because Beccaria perceived the penal system as responsible for punishing offenders but rejected the idea that any penal system was invested of the power to revenge a crime through the use of extreme violence. Beccaria's principles were welcomed across Europe (especially in France and England), criticized in Germany (mostly by Kant and Hegel), and endorsed in America. It was noted that Thomas Jefferson "copied whole pages of the work into his diary and drew on it in his effort to abolish the death penalty" (Harcourt, 2013: 4).

The idea of "compassion" is central to our understanding of Beccaria's ideology. He debated that punishment should not be pursued for petty offenses which often stem from necessity rather than from malicious intent. He believed that social disorganization and poverty could be reduced by spreading education among the masses (Beccaria, 1764). European penal reformers, such as Blackstone, often applied Beccaria's principles selectively. For instance, while endorsing Beccaria's ideas, Blackstone, an English penal reformer, maintained a strong support for the death penalty (Draper, 2000).

Beccaria was an egalitarian who believed that no justice can be achieved unless all men are considered equal before the law. He rejected elitist ideologies in that he believed that wealth tends to feed tyranny (Beccaria, 1764).

UTILITARIANISM

Beccaria's work strongly influenced Jeremy Bentham's theory of utilitarianism. In his 1789 "An Introduction to the Principles of Morals and Legislation" Bentham explained that for crime to be an effective deterrent of future crime, punishment must hurt the hedonic nature of the offender. Within the "hedonic calculus" model, punishment was determined as a proportion of both the pleasure the offender gained through the crime committed and the social pain caused to others by that crime (Burns, 2005).

Bentham believed that punishment had to be identified on the basis of the offender's motive, circumstance, and intention to harm (Draper, 2000). In this, Bentham's theory appears more sophisticated than Beccaria's, and it is believed that Bentham provided the most significant contribution to the utilitarian proportion theory (Draper, 2000).

Within the utilitarian view, preventing crime is more important than punishment per se. The focus is on the criminal act rather than the individual. Because the individual is considered rational within utilitarianism, punishment must be used for the purpose of discouraging crime from re-occurring. The certainty of punishment and its discomfort became central to the design of institutional punishment. Bentham developed a plan for a penitentiary known as "panopticon." As the word suggests (*pan*=all and *optikon*=view), this type of penitentiary would allow for the exercise of complete control over the offender. A central tower of circular shape with cells built all around the circumference on each story of the building would make constant surveillance of all inmates possible at all time (Clear, Reisig, & Cole, 2016; Foucault, 1977; Newman, 1985). Although never adopted in Europe, the panopticon was developed in the United States in both Pennsylvania and Illinois. However, it was, abandoned very quickly because considered too oppressive (Clear, Reisig, & Cole, 2016; Foucault, 1977).

While the focus on reason characterized much of the discourse around crime and punishment during the 18th century, the 19th-century ideals shifted the focus from reason to morality and moral law became the central element in the determination of punishment.

GERMAN IDEALISM

In 1887, Immanuel Kant published "The Philosophy of Law" in which he debated that people have an absolute duty to obey moral law as the universal moral principle. For Kant, everyone in society benefits from obeying the rule of law. Conformity to social norms is what grants happiness to society as a whole. Punishment for those who attempt to gain unfair advantage over others' happiness is necessary to restore the order within a society; it is only through punishment that the right of the offender to be part of the same community he wronged can be restored (Clarke, 1982).

In his analysis of German idealism, Clarke (1982) argued that punishment is either deterrent or retributive but cannot be both. While Kant supported the idea of retributive punishment, he did not necessarily disagree with utilitarianism either; however, he made a clear distinction between the *real* (positive law or reasons of deterrence and prevention) and the *ideal* (moral law). Kant argued that only when positive law coincides with moral law (as a system of beliefs shared by all members of society), we have an effective form of punishment. While the goal of punishment for any ruling authority is broader (deterrence/prevention), at the individual level, punishment works as the infliction of moral guilt. Punishment per se is not beneficial to society unless it is effective for the sinner. Kant rejected the pragmatism of utility theory, in that no one should ever profit or benefit from punishment. Punishment is necessary to punish the accused, but it does not serve the purpose of the greater good. For Kant, punishment is good in itself (Clarke, 1982).

Like Kant, Hegel rejected Beccaria's idea of social contract and the "immorality" of utilitarianism. Hegel's retributive theory focuses on the idea that individuals are granted the right to choose; when they choose to wrong society, they have the "right" to receive a punishment. In Hegel's ideal, punishment as retribution is a form of respect of the individual. Hegel opposes utilitarianism because he believes it reduces humans to animals as they obey the moral law only because of their fear of punishment. The main difference between the German idealism and utilitarianism lies in the nature of punishment itself; the first centered on a transcendental and religious moralism (idealistic form of punishment), the second focused on secular humanism and pragmatism (contractual nature of punishment) (Clarke, 1982).

© kavalenkau/Shutterstock.com

Monument to the famous doctor, anthropologist, and criminologist Cesare Lombroso set in Verona.

BIOLOGICAL DETERMINISM AND POSITIVISM

Theories of evolution had a major influence on the explanation of crime and punishment that developed throughout the 19th and 20th centuries. With the publication of Charles Darwin's "On the Origins of Species" in 1860, new theories on human behavior became dominant (Mazzarello, 2011).

In Italy, Cesare Lombroso, a prominent doctor and influential intellectual, applied evolution to the study of criminals. Lombroso believed that delinquents shared common physical traits (especially the shape of the forehead and the cranium) that resembled primitive humans. In his most influential book, "The Criminal Man," published in 1876, Lombroso explained that criminals were "throwbacks" whose mental development stopped early, remaining at the primitive stage (a phenomenon also known as *atavism*). He described various features commonly found among delinquent men in Italy: small cranium, large ears, and darker skin. Lombroso theories of delinquency became known among criminologists as "biological determinism." Biological determinism developed within the context of positivist criminology, an ideology that became popular between 1826 and 1829 with the Belgian statistician Adolphe Quetelet. Positivism was considered as an innovative approach to the study of crime in that it offered empirical explanations of social observations (Winslow & Zhang, 2008).

While Lombroso's theories would today be dismissed as racist propaganda, at the turn of the 20th century, they had a strong influence on the political discourse and implementation of fascist policies focusing on the idea of racial purity as an element of nationalism (Winslow & Zhang, 2008). Lombroso's theories of biological determinism, which aimed to provide the guidelines for identifying and isolating the born criminals, were welcome among the supporters of the eugenics movement that sought to create a selective breeding in the United States between the 1920s and through the 1940s (Winslow & Zhang, 2008). Lombroso was criticized for exclusively focusing on the features of the individual, omitting almost completely the influence of social and economic factors affecting the delinquent men and women he studied (Ferri, 1917). While pioneering the application of the scientific method to study delinquency and criminality was seen as a major contribution in Lombroso's work, the limitations of his sampling methodologies made his results biased and unreliable (Mazzarello, 2011).

A commonality across all the philosophies of punishment explored in this chapter is the search for a justification for punishment. While punishment is unequivocally seen as a necessary means to maintain social order, thinkers have always been troubled by the questions on its effectiveness and fairness. In "The Division of Labor in Society," Durkheim and Simpson (1993) argued that punishment is used in every society to reinforce the solidarity of the group. Punishment has the ultimate goal to reaffirm the social consciousness shared among most members of society (Spietzer, 1975).

Utilitarianism, German Idealism, Biological Determinism and Positivism all influenced the U.S. penal system in different moments of the history of the United States. Chapter 3 provides an overview of different eras within the history of U.S. corrections. The underlying principles of those movements are found in the philosophies of punishment explained in this chapter.

LEARNING EXERCISES

- Create a chronology of the various philosophies of punishment that dominated the field of penology during the 18th and 19th centuries Europe.
- Articulate the differences between utilitarianism and German idealism.
- Identify common elements in all the theories of punishment discussed in the chapter.

BIBLIOGRAPHY

Beccaria, C. (1764). Dei delitti e delle pene. *Opera immortale, Vienna, Sam*.

Clarke, D. H. (1982). Justifications for punishment. *Contemporary Crises*, 6(1), 25–57.

Clear, T., Reisig, M., & Cole, G. (2016). *American corrections* (11th ed.). Boston, MA: Cengage Learning.

Draper, A. J. (2000). Cesare Beccaria's influence on English discussions of punishment, 1764–1789. *History of European Ideas*, 26(3), 177–199.

Durkheim, E., & Simpson, G. (1933). *The division of labor in Society*. New York, NY: Macmillan.

Foucault, M. (1977). *Discipline and punish: The birth of the prison*. Trans. Sheridan A. London: Penguin Books.

Harcourt, B. E. (2013). Beccaria's' On Crimes and Punishments': A Mirror on the History of the Foundations of Modern Criminal Law. *Political Law and Legal Theory* Working Papers. University of Chicago Law School, Chicago, IL.

Mazzarello, P. (2011). Cesare Lombroso: An anthropologist between evolution and degeneration. *Functional Neurology*, 26(2), 97–101.

Newman, G. R. (1985). *The punishment response*. Albany, NY: Transaction publishers.

Winslow, R. W., & Zhang, S. (2008). *Criminology: A global perspective*. Boston: Pearson Prentice Hall.

CHAPTER 3

Goals of Punishment and Corrections

Archway Migdal Tsedek Tower of Justice National park

LEARNING OBJECTIVES

- Discuss the influence of Utilitarianism, German Idealism, and Positivism on the modern goals of punishment and corrections

- Explain, compare, and contrast the goals of deterrence, incapacitation, rehabilitation, retribution, and restitution

- Articulate the main characteristics of the restorative justice model

INTRODUCTION

Chapter 2 presented an overview of philosophies that continue to influence the U.S. system of punishment and corrections. Principles of utilitarianism, German Idealism, and positivism have all influenced the U.S. political discourse and the different eras and movements that led to penal reforms. Within each movement, a different ideology dominated the field of corrections. For instance, during the first half of the 19th century, throughout the Jackson's era, rehabilitation was considered a main goal of corrections. However, because the use of solitary confinement did not help rehabilitate offenders, the attention shifted toward incapacitation very quickly (Kifer, Hemmens, & Stohr, 2003; Rothman, 1971). Later, from the 1870s through the 1970s, rehabilitation became the main goal of corrections (Clear, Reisig, & Cole, 2016; Oliver & Hilgenberg, 2010). The era following the dissolution of the rehabilitation movement is known for its emphasis on the retributive nature of punishment. Today, the key principles of the philosophies discussed in Chapter 2 coexist within a modern and complex system of punishment and corrections. Table 3.1 provides an overview of the goals of corrections in association with the doctrines discussed in Chapter 2.

Table 3.1 Dominant philosophies and goals of punishment and corrections

Dominant philosophy	Goals of punishment and corrections
Utilitarianism	Deterrence (specific and general)
	Incapacitation
	Rehabilitation
German Idealism	Retribution
Positivism	Incapacitation
	Rehabilitation

Note: Not all criminologists agree that rehabilitation can exist at the same time as incapacitation.

DETERRENCE

Within the philosophy of utilitarianism, the main purpose of punishment is prevention. To be effective, punishment must be certain and severe and it must be proportionate to the crime committed. An effective punishment, within the utilitarian view, is a punishment that prevents the offender from repeating an offense (*specific deterrence*) and at the same time, discourages others from engaging in criminal activities (*general deterrence*). By punishing the offender, the State provides an example of how those who break the law are held accountable for the harm they have caused to others (Beccaria, 1764; Burns, 2005).

In the U.S. Criminal Justice System, deterrence is the primary goal of punishment. However, extant studies on the effect of punishment on recidivism show that, even in its most severe form (death penalty), punishment in the United States has not produced the intended effect (Donohue III & Wolfers, 2006; Wright, 2010). One of the major limitations of punishment as deterrent is that it assumes that crime stems from rational behavior (Burns, 2005).

Empirical studies show that many offenders suffer from mental disabilities or substance abuse problems, issues that could potentially prevent individuals from making rational decisions (Wright, 2010).

INCAPACITATION

The goal of incapacitation in punishment and corrections stems from the idea that by limiting an offender's personal liberties it is possible to prevent that any further harm is done to society. In many cultures throughout history, offenders were isolated from the rest of society via banishment or exile (Ekirch, 1985). Modern forms of incapacitation tend to target specific types of offenders (see for instance sex-offenders) and create barriers to prevent the offender from hurting society any further (Yung, 2007). Incapacitation is often used within the prison system to isolate offenders who are deemed dangerous and unable to share common space with other inmates.

The goal of incapacitation in punishment is present in both the utilitarian philosophy and positivism. Within the utilitarian view, the need for isolating the offender is fully represented in Bentham's design of the penitentiary (Foucault, 1977; Newman, 1985). However, in Positivism, incapacitation refers to the isolation of potential offenders before they commit crime. An example of this approach can be found in the Eugenics laws (Winslow & Zhang, 2008) and in the confinement of Japanese Americans during World War II (Materni, 2013). These are obviously extreme examples of preemptive incapacitation that cannot be accommodated in a democratic social and political system (Materni, 2013).

REHABILITATION

The goal of rehabilitation stems from principles of both utilitarianism and positivism. A compassionate approach to punishment was central to Beccaria's philosophy of punishment, especially for offenses that appeared to be directly associated with the offender's needs rather than his malice (Beccaria, 1764). Because positivism focused on the idea that crime is the result of the individual's characteristics, the search for treatment became a key element in the design and implementation of punishment. In addition, identifying forms of punishment that would fit the individual's needs became a primary goal within this philosophy. This individual-centered philosophy of punishment would translate into a more complex court system where the evidence of a crime must also include a complete discussion around the offender's traits and needs (Foucault, 1977).

The modern mission of corrections in the United States includes both punishment and rehabilitation. The U.S. Bureau of Prisons, for instance, includes rehabilitation in the agency's mission statement (U.S. Bureau of Prisons, 2017). While some argue that rehabilitation appears in contradiction with the inhumane conditions in which many offenders are forced to live, the two goals coexist in the U.S. modern criminal justice system (Materni, 2013).

Throughout much of the 20th century, in the United States, rehabilitation was contemplated in various forms, through both medical interventions (during the medical era) and community-based intervention (during the reintegration era that followed the civil rights' movements). Different rehabilitation models were implemented across the country, each targeting a different aspect of the offenders' needs, his relationship with his family, his interpersonal relationships, and the community, in addition to physical and psychological needs (Stinchcomb, 2002). However, by the mid-1970s, the rehabilitation model had failed, and after the publication of Martison's "What Works?" in 1974, it was quickly dismissed because inadequate. While it can be argued that Martison was misunderstood, the publication of his exploratory work became a catalyst for the beginning of the "nothing works" movement against the use of rehabilitative measures. One of the main problems with the existing rehabilitation programs was that they were often not implemented according to their original design (Petersilia, 2004).

RETRIBUTION

The goal of retribution stems from the German Idealism tradition of punishment. For both Kant and Hegel, punishment was a form of revenge against those who wronged society. Punishment had the ultimate goal to punish the individual and punishment was good in itself (Clarke, 1982). In the retributive ideal, punishment is defined within the interpretation of moral law and it has the sole purpose of hurting one's human dignity (Materni, 2013).

From the beginning of the 1980s, the focus on rehabilitation was replaced by an emphasis on punishment as *just desert* (just what one deserves). This new era in the U.S. system of punishment and corrections is often known as the "tough on crime" era. Stiffer penalties were introduced for almost every crime with new sentencing models that allowed for lengthier and more severe forms of punishment. Today, many criminologists believe that this new focus on retribution during the last several decades has contributed to the mass incarceration of many young Americans (Stinchcomb, 2002).

RESTITUTION AND RESTORATIVE JUSTICE

Although the idea of restitution was introduced only recently in the U.S. system of punishment and corrections, restitution and restorative justice have existed in all the civilizations throughout the history of human kind as we know it (Umbreit, Coates, & Kalanj, 1994). Based on the idea that the offender should be provided with the opportunity to repay the victim, the victim's family, and the community, restorative justice is a very distinctive form of punishment (Sherman & Strang, 2007).

Restorative justice models employ a circular method of resolution; in other words, the offender sits in a circle together with members of the community and figures representing the criminal justice system to brainstorm about strategies and programs that would help reinstate the social balance that the offense disrupted. The restorative justice model requires that the community becomes involved in finding a resolution; it also requires full commitment from the offender. Studies show that restorative justice can be more successful than other justice models in reducing recidivism (Braithwaite, 2016). Restorative justice programs are beginning to be implemented also in some schools and local communities to prevent the occurrence of crime (Gonzalez, 2012). The implementation of restorative justice programs has been successful in other countries as well (Winfree, 2002).

In summary, while utilitarianism, German Idealism, and positivism have all influenced the U.S. system of punishment and corrections throughout history, the U.S. criminal justice system today employs all these principles at the same time. When taken all together, the various goals of punishment and corrections reviewed in this chapter become an integral part of the current system of checks and balances (Materni, 2013).

LEARNING ACTIVITIES

- Create a chart in which you map the different eras/movements of justice in the United States throughout the 19th and 20th centuries by connecting them to specific goals of punishment and corrections prioritized in each era.
- In an essay, reflect on the various goals of corrections and provide examples of how these goals coexist in our modern system of punishment.

BIBLIOGRAPHY

Beccaria, C. (1764). Dei delitti e delle pene. *Opera immortale, Vienna, Sam.*

Braithwaite, J. B. (2016). Restorative Justice and Responsive Regulation: The Question of Evidence. RegNet Research Paper No. 2014/51. Available at SSRN: https://ssrn.com/abstract=2514127 or http://dx.doi.org/10.2139/ssrn.2514127

Burns, J. H. (2005). Happiness and utility: Jeremy Bentham's equation. *Utilitas, 17*(1), 46–61.

Clarke, D. H. (1982). Justifications for punishment. *Contemporary Crises, 6*(1), 25–57.

Clear, T., Reisig, M., & Cole, G. (2016). *American corrections* (11th ed.). Boston, MA: Cengage Learning.

Donohue III, J. J., & Wolfers, J. (2006). *Uses and abuses of empirical evidence in the death penalty debate* (No. w11982). National Bureau of Economic Research.

Ekirch, A. R. (1985). Bound for America: A profile of British convicts transported to the colonies, 1718–1775. *The William and Mary Quarterly: A Magazine of Early American History,* pp. 184–200.

Foucault, M. (1977). *Discipline and punish: The birth of the prison.* Trans. Sheridan A. London: Penguin Books.

Gonzalez, T. (2012). Keeping kids in schools: Restorative justice, punitive discipline, and the school to prison pipeline. *Journal of Law & Education, 41*(2), 281–335.

Kifer, M., Hemmens, C., & Stohr, M. K. (2003). The goals of corrections: Perspectives from the line. *Criminal Justice Review, 28*(1), 47–69.

Materni, M. C. (2013). Criminal punishment and the pursuit of justice. *British Journal of American Legal Studies, 2,* 263.

Newman, G. R. (1985). *The punishment response.* Albany, NY: Transaction publishers.

Oliver, W. M., & Hilgenberg, J. F. (2010). *A history of crime and criminal justice in America.* Carolina Academic Press.

Petersilia, J. (2004). What works in prisoner reentry-reviewing and questioning the evidence. *Federal Probation Journal, 68,* 4.

Rothman, D. 1971. *The discovery of the asylum: Social order and disorder in the new republic*. Boston: Little, Brown.

Sherman, L., & Strang, H. (2007). *Restorative justice: The evidence*. Smith Institute.

Stinchcomb, J. B. (2002). From rehabilitation to retribution: Examining public policy paradigms and personnel education patterns in corrections. *American Journal of Criminal Justice*, 27(1), 1–17.

Umbreit, M. S., Coates, R. B., & Kalanj, B. (1994). *Victim meets offender: The impact of restorative justice and mediation* (pp. 53–64). Monsey, NY: Criminal Justice Press.

U.S. Bureau of Prisons (2017). Mission. Available at: https://www.bop.gov/about/agency/agency_pillars.jsp last visited on 11-05-2017.

Winfree Jr, L. T. (2002). Peacemaking and community harmony: Lessons (and admonitions) from the Navajo peacemaking courts. In E. G. M. Weitekamp, & H.-J. Kerner (Eds.), *Restorative justice: Theoretical foundations* (pp. 285–307). New York, NY: Willan Publishing.

Winslow, R. W., & Zhang, S. (2008). *Criminology: A global perspective*. Upper Saddle River, NJ, Pearson Prentice Hall.

Wright, V. (2010). *Deterrence in criminal justice: Evaluating certainty vs. severity of punishment*. Sentencing Project.

Yung, C. R. (2007). Banishment by a thousand laws: Residency restrictions on sex offenders. *Washington University Law Review*, 85, 101.

Race and Punishment in the United States

Nocturnal gathering of robed and hooded Ku Klux Klan men in 1921–1922. Photo by National Photo Company and was likely taken within 100 miles of Washington, D.C.

In 1998, James W. Clarke conducted a study on the issue of racial disparities in the U.S. system of punishment. Clarke's investigation focused on the years between 1882 and 1962. The study, published in the *British Journal of Political Science*, specifically addressed the problem of both informal and formal punishment in the southern states of the country (Alabama, Arkansas, Florida, Georgia, Kentucky, Louisiana, Maryland, Mississippi, Missouri, North Carolina, South Carolina, Tennessee, Texas, Virginia).

Examples of lynching, burning, and public executions are described in the study to represent practices that continued to be used in the South of the United States even after the 1863 Emancipation Proclamation issued by President Abraham Lincoln. As Clarke (1998) reveals, lynching was not a rare event in the South during slavery, but it was most often used to punish whites for murder or other serious offenses, like for instance, stealing livestock or hurting another white man's slaves. During that time, lynching was used when justice authorities (the local sheriff or the judge) were out of reach.

In his analysis, Clarke found that "a new era of lynching began in that year [1868] when the Ku Klux Klan killed at least 291 black males and left countless other men, women, and children physically and psychologically maimed by brutal beatings and sexual mutilations" (Clarke, 1998: 271). During the time the KKK took punishment in its own hands, blacks could expect to be victimized anywhere and anytime. They could be lynched for any reason either real of fabricated. Even when blacks were under the surveillance of police officers, the KKK could intervene and exercise revenge for crimes blacks were accused of, even if no arrest had been made. Indifference was widespread across institutions as police officers, mayors, or even the clergy looked the other way. The lynching of blacks, in a swift manner, was widely accepted and justified by thousands of whites from all walks of life in the South.

By examining archived newspaper records and data collected by the Alabama Department of Records and Research of the Tuskegee Institute, Clarke found that between 1882 and 1962 a total of 3,875 people were lynched in the former slave states. Among them, 3,264 were blacks (84% of all victims). An important point to be made is that, at that time, blacks represented only 29% of the general population of those states.

When data on capital punishment (formal punishment exercised by the state) was taken into consideration, Clarke's analysis revealed that racial discrimination has been a regional pattern ever since "records have been kept" (Clarke, 1998: 286). By combining the deaths of those who were lynched by the mob with the deaths of those who were executed by the state, Clarke found that 75% of all the offenders put to death were blacks. Clarke's explains the findings of his research through the lens of Wolfgang's and Ferracuti's *Theory of Subculture of Violence*. In Clarke's words, "perhaps the most convincing support for the theory rests on two facts: the almost complete impunity with which such atrocities occurred; and, secondly, that lynching's decline was hastened by a pernicious system of court-ordered executions that served the same purpose" (Clarke, 1998, p. 289).

BIBLIOGRAPHY

Clarke, J. W. (1998). Without fear or shame: Lynching, capital punishment and the subculture of violence in the American South. *British Journal of Political Science*, 28(2), 269–289.

Section II

Sentencing

Symbol of law and justice on the table, law and justice concept, focus on the scales, blue tone

CHAPTER 4

The Criminal Justice System in Review

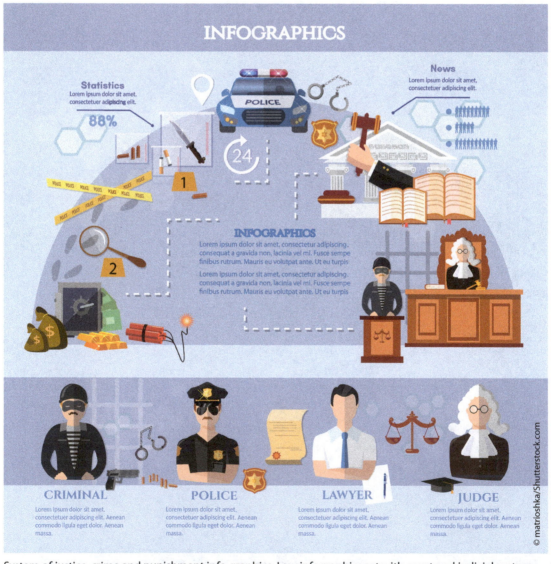

System of justice, crime and punishment info graphics. Law infographics set with court and judicial system elements vector illustration.

LEARNING OBJECTIVES

- Discuss current perspectives on the rise in number of convictions experienced in the last 40 years

- Articulate the objectives of the War on Drugs and its overall impact on poor communities

- Summarize the current scenario in sentencing and corrections

INTRODUCTION

In the 1970s, the United States began to experience an increase in rates of arrest, conviction, and incarceration that continued through the first decade of the 21st century. Franklin Zimring, a leader in crime analysis, identified three distinct phases in the rise of incarceration across the nation (Simon, 2012). The first phase, between 1970 and 1985, characterized by changes in prosecutorial practices that allowed for assigning prison sentences to low profile felons, rather than sending them to jail for a short period of time, or sentencing them to a period of probation. The second phase, between 1985 and 1995, characterized by the implementation of new laws that mandated the criminalization of drug offenses and authorized states to adapt mandatory minimums to extend prison sentences. The third phase, between 1995 and 2005, characterized by the implementation of new policies that allowed states to make statutory changes to limit the early release of offenders (such as *truth-in sentences* and *three-strike-and-you-are-out* policies) (Simon, 2012; Zimring, 2010). The increase in the number of felons throughout the three phases identified by Zimring occurred during a time in which crime rates continued to fall at an unprecedented rate all across the United States (Zimring, 2010).

Looking at the bigger picture, Wacquant (2009) discusses the connection between mass-incarceration and changes in the economy. With new advances in technology and the decline of the manufacturing sector throughout the Western Hemisphere, large numbers of unemployable individuals have become inconvenient to the technocrats who exploit social control policies to marginalize those not fully engaged within the innovations of the labor market. Reading through Wacquant's analysis, it appears that the penal system has replaced the welfare state

Equal Justice For All is an illustration of a design depicting the concept of equal justice for everyone. Done in a striking black and white for emphasis.

© AWesleyFloyd/Shutterstock.com

by governing the poor while creating new business for the private economic sector (Beckett & Western, 2001; Simon, 2012), an approach that Davis discusses as "carceral Keynesianism" (Davis, 1990; Simon, 2012).

Another perspective on the expansion of the penal system targets the use of "fear of crime" in political narrative as a demagogical tool for American politicians of both the Republican and Democratic parties throughout the 1980s and 1990s (Lynch, 2009). Although the idea of locking up criminals has always been considered part of a conservative political agenda, voters from both the left and the right sides of the political spectrum have supported the rhetoric that crime and criminals represent a major threat to the public safety in their communities. By supporting policies that emphasized fear of crime, U.S. voters have over time allowed the capitalistic regime to benefit from the expansion of the penal system and control minorities. While mass-incarceration is no longer a supported public policy, there are many reasons to believe that prisons will remain a viable solution for the control of the poor in many metropolitan areas of the United States (Simon, 2012).

RACIAL DISPARITIES IN SENTENCING

To understand the impact of criminal justice policies implemented in the United States between 1970 and 2010, one must revisit theories of inequality and the history of race relations (Reiman & Leighton, 2015). Issues associated with social disorganization in large metropolitan areas have contributed to the marginalization of poor minorities in urban neighborhoods (Massey & Denton, 1989). In addition, it is important to analyze how police tactics and judicial practices employed by criminal justice agencies influence the representation of minority groups in institutions of punishment and corrections (Davis, 1996). Criminologist Michael Tonry points out that "sentencing decisions by judges are not a major contributor to racial disparities" (2012: 55). A review of studies on the disparities of sentencing practices in the United States shows that minority defendants are not more likely than white defendants to be sentenced to a prison term for violent crimes; however, blacks are more likely than whites to receive a prison sentence for both drug offenses and property offenses (Demuth & Steffensmeier, 2004; Tonry, 2012). In addition, research shows that black defendants are, on average, more likely to receive longer prison terms than white defendants (Kautt & Spohn, 2002; Tonry, 2012). Police practices implemented in metropolitan areas to crack down drug operations have produced high numbers of arrestees among black youth (Brunson, 2007). Arrest rates by race appear to be in contradiction with the findings of national surveys suggesting that whites in the United States consume and sell drugs at higher rates than minorities (Johnston, O'Malley, Bachman, & Schulenberg, 2013). As Tonry (2012) points out, blacks, however, are more likely to sell and use drugs in places where it is easier to be surveilled by the police and be arrested. While traditionally blacks were primarily incarcerated for their involvement in violent crimes, this is no longer the case because rates of violent crime among blacks continue to fall (Tonry, 2012). Instead, racial profiling and drug laws contribute to police tactics that target poor minorities, especially in low-income black communities. In Tonry's words, "[f]or most serious crimes, the crime itself appeared to be the primary factor explaining sentencing decisions, leaving comparatively little room for bias or stereotyping to operate. Less serious crimes

RIO DE JANEIRO, Brazil May, 04th, 2017 Anti-riot policemen searches a truck looking for drugs at the Alemao shatytown entrance after a confrontation with drug lords that resulted in 5 deaths.

allowed more room for discretionary decision making and the crime itself explained less" (Tonry, 2012: 64).

THE WAR ON DRUGS LEGISLATION

"War on drugs" is a term used to identify a complex body of laws primarily targeting the supply side of the drug enterprise implemented between the late 1970s and the first decade of the 21st century across five different U.S. presidential administrations. Because illicit drugs are mostly produced in poor economies, the U.S. government has systematically targeted supplying countries in an attempt to eradicate the production of heroin, cocaine, and marijuana. Three strategies were used to eliminate drugs from the U.S. market: First, the United States pressured supplying countries to impose crop-substitution plans to eliminate the production of illegal drugs. This imposition created dissent and rebel groups formed to protect the production of illegal substances (drug cartels). Second, the U.S. government intensified control of the borders and of all the movement of people and goods from and to other countries. Third, the U.S. government implemented tough on crime policies to monitor illegal activities occurring within the country. Both at the federal and local levels, police departments across the country implemented tactics to interfere with gang criminal activities focused on the distribution of drugs. By attacking the supply side of the drug market, U.S. policies contributed to the increased risk for all parties involved in the illegal enterprise of an underground market. Reducing the supply of the drugs and increasing the risk of arrest, conviction, and detention for those caught while engaging in drug distribution operations forced the price to go up, making dealing and distributing drugs an incredibly profitable business (Bertram, 1996).

In addition to creating huge unanticipated consequences in the expansion of the drug market, both within the United States and abroad, the War on Drugs contributed to the disparity in sentencing between black and white defendants (Tonry, 2012). Examples of drug laws that disproportionately punish blacks still exist in the United States. The 1986 "100 to 1" law specifically punished the sales of crack 100 times more than the sales of cocaine, in spite the fact that the two substances are made of the same pharmacological components (Reinarman & Levine, 2004). President Obama later modified the law by reducing the ratio crack-cocaine to "18 to 1" in 2008. While this ratio appears to be less discriminating, the difference between crack and cocaine still reflects the prejudice surrounding the use of crack (predominantly by poor minorities) when compared to the use of cocaine (predominantly by whites).

TRENDS IN SENTENCING AND CORRECTIONS

Using data from the Bureau of Justice Statistics, Tonry (2012) provided us with an overview of the impact of the War on Drugs' legislation on sentencing disparities in black America. While in the 1960s blacks represented 36% of those incarcerated, 50% of the inmates in U.S. correctional facilities were blacks by mid-1980s. The percentage of minorities in prison must be compared to the percentage of minorities in society. Because black Americans make up for 13.3% of the U.S. population (U.S. Census, 2010), one would expect to see a similar proportion of blacks in prison. However, discriminatory policies that prescribed tougher sentences for the use and distribution of drugs most commonly used among poor blacks (specifically crack), contributed to the disproportionate representation of blacks in the U.S. criminal justice system (Reinarman & Levine, 2004).

The overall rate of imprisonment in the 1970s in the United States was 161 per 100,000 residents, while for blacks the rate of imprisonment was 593 per 100,000 residents. By 2010, the overall imprisonment rate had increased from 161 to 780 per 100,000 residents. However, for blacks rates of incarceration had moved from 593 to 2,661 per 100,000 residents in 2006 (Tonry, 2012: 57). While some changes have been observed more recently, blacks are still overrepresented within the U.S. system of punishment and corrections (Tonry, 2012).

Current estimates indicate that blacks represent roughly 13% of the U.S. population and 40% of all the inmates in prisons and jails. Latinos and Hispanics represent 16% of the U.S. population and 19% of those locked up in prisons and jails. Whites represent 64% of the U.S. population but only 39% of the overall inmate population in prisons and jails (Wagner & Rabuy, 2017). These disparities still reflect the effect of drug policies but it is important to remember that the War on Drugs also resulted in an increase in rates of violent crime, driven especially by turf battles that aim at protecting a gang's share of the market within communities and neighborhoods (Block & Block, 1993).

Today, incarceration represents only a fraction of the total number of people under correctional supervision. Estimates of the Prison Policy Initiative show that, in 2017, there were 7 million people under the supervision of the American correctional system, of whom

3.7 million were on probation, 2.3 million were incarcerated in prison, jails, or detention facilities, and 840,000 were completing their sentence on parole (Wagner & Rabuy, 2017). Bureau of Justice Statistics' estimates (Kaeble, Maruschak, & Bonczar, 2015) show that one every 53 adults in the United States are under the supervision of the criminal justice system in the community.

Women still represent a small fraction of the total sentencing and corrections population of the United States. Studies show that, on average, women are less likely than men to become incarcerated; in addition, women also tend to receive shorter sentences than men (Clear, Reisig, & Cole, 2018; Spohn, 2009). However, studies' findings show that the influence of demographics like race and age also contribute to the differences between the sentences male and female offenders receive in court (Spohn, 2009). Judges tend to be more lenient toward female offenders than toward male offenders but this is true only for women conforming to traditional gender roles (Koons-Witt, 2002). Current estimates show that there are 219,000 women incarcerated in jails and prisons. In addition, 60% of the women confined in jails are awaiting adjudication. This is most often due to their inability to pay bail, as incarcerated women tend to be very poor. These statistics are particularly alarming because incarcerated women are more likely than their male counterpart to be solely responsible for their children (Wagner & Rabuy, 2017).

LEARNING EXERCISES

Essay Questions:

- What are the main perspectives that explain the focus on crime and punishment of the last 50 years?
- What are the various ways in which the War on Drugs legislation impacted both local and international communities?
- What are your main observations about the current trend in the U.S. system of punishment and corrections? Can you discuss race and gender disparities?

BIBLIOGRAPHY

Beckett, K., & Western, B. (2001). Governing social marginality: Welfare, incarceration, and the transformation of state policy. *Punishment & Society*, *3*(1), 43–59.

Bertram, E. (1996). *Drug war politics: The price of denial*. Berkeley, CA: Univ of California Press.

Block, C. R., & Block, R. (1993). *Street gang crime in Chicago* (pp. 1–8). Washington, DC: US Department of Justice, Office of Justice Programs, National Institute of Justice.

Brunson, R. K. (2007). "Police don't like black people": African-American young men's accumulated police experiences. *Criminology & Public Policy*, *6*(1), 71–101.

Clear, T. R., Reisig, M. D., & Cole, G. F. (2018). *American corrections*. Boston, MA: Cengage Learning.

Davis, M. (2006). *City of Quartz: Excavating the Future in Los Angeles (New Edition)*. New York, NY: Verso Books.

Demuth, S., & Steffensmeier, D. (2004). Ethnicity effects on sentence outcomes in large urban courts: Comparisons among White, Black, and Hispanic defendants. *Social Science Quarterly*, *85*(4), 994–1011.

Johnston, L. D., O'Malley, P. M., Bachman, J. G., & Schulenberg, J. E. (2013). *Monitoring the Future national results on adolescent drug use: Overview of key findings, 2012*. Bethesda, MD: National Institute on Drug Abuse.

Kaeble, D., Maruschak, L. M., & Bonczar, T. P. (2015). *Probation and parole in the United States, 2014*. Washington, DC: Bureau of Justice Statistics (BJS), U.S. Department of Justice, and Office of Justice Programs.

Kautt, P., & Spohn, C. (2002). Crack-ing down on black drug offenders? Testing for interactions among offenders' race, drug type, and sentencing strategy in federal drug sentences. *Justice Quarterly*, *19*(1), 1–35.

Koons-Witt, B. A. (2002). The effect of gender on the decision to incarcerate before and after the introduction of sentencing guidelines. *Criminology*, *40*(2), 297–328.

Lynch, M. (2009). *Sunbelt justice: Arizona and the transformation of American punishment*. Stanford, CA: Stanford University Press.

Massey, D. S., & Denton, N. A. (1989). Hypersegregation in US metropolitan areas: Black and Hispanic segregation along five dimensions. *Demography*, *26*(3), 373–391.

Reinarman, C., & Levine, H. G. (2004). Crack in the rearview mirror: Deconstructing drug war mythology. *Social Justice*, *31*(1/2) (95–96), 182–199.

Reiman, J., & Leighton, P. (2015). *The rich get richer and the poor get prison: Ideology, class, and criminal justice*. New York, NY: Routledge.

Simon, J. (2012). Mass incarceration: From social policy to social problem. In J. Petersilia, & K. R. Reitz (Eds.), *The Oxford handbook of sentencing and corrections* (pp. 23–52). New York, NY: Oxford Univ Press,.

Spohn, C. (2009). *How do judges decide? The search for fairness and justice in punishment*. Thousand Oaks: CA: SAGE Publications Inc.

Zimring, F. E. (2010). The scale of imprisonment in the United States: Twentieth century patterns and twenty-first century prospects. *The Journal of Criminal Law and Criminology (1973–)*, *100*(3), 1225–1246.

Wacquant, L. (2009). *Punishing the poor: The neoliberal government of social insecurity*. Durham: Duke University Press.

Wagner, P., & Rabuy, B. (2017). Mass incarceration: The whole pie 2016 [press release]. Prison Policy Initiative.

CHAPTER 5

Sentencing Processes

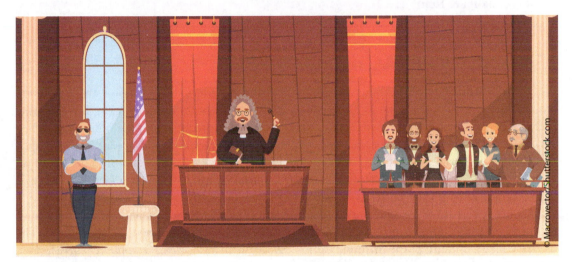

American court of law judicial legal proceedings in courthouse with judge and jury box retro poster illustration

LEARNING OBJECTIVES

- Explain the current scenario of the U.S. criminal court system
- Articulate the processes that sentence offenders
- Compare different sentencing models within the U.S. penal system

INTRODUCTION

In the United States, the two fields of sentencing and corrections are interconnected. Sentencing is the legal process through which a disciplinary action is prescribed for an offender following a violation of the law. However, any sentence is abstract in its essence until its full implementation and administration within correctional institutions (Petersilia & Reitz, 2012).

A glance at correctional practices would suggest that any decision reached in the courtroom is followed by a number of adjustments that are based on the offenders' risks and needs upon their entrance into the correctional system. In addition, such adjustments are also determined based on the offender's behavior while under the supervision of the criminal justice system. Finally, many decisions are finalized based on the availability of resources, such as the availability of reentry and rehabilitation programs aimed at preparing the offender to return to the community after a period of incarceration. Sentencing decisions often follow the offender even after punishment is completed. The consequences of criminal sanctions tend to stain one's reputation and ability to gain back one's access to social, economic, and political power (Chin, 2002; Chesney-Lind & Mauer, 2003; Pinard, 2006; Travis, 2002).

While corrections experts are fully invested in the assessment and explanation of every aspect of sentencing as experienced within the U.S. penal system, society is mostly interested in the court's fairness and ability to restore justice in the community after an offender is punished (Petersilia & Reitz, 2012).

SENTENCING PRACTICES

As a former British colony, the United States inherited the English Common Law tradition in which the judge is at the center of the adversarial system. In its modern form, however, the U.S. adversarial process emphasizes the role of both the prosecutor and the defense attorney. As Wright (2012) explains, the charges, evidence, and remedial options tend to be shaped through the decisions of the two parties. Sentencing practices are defined within the broad set of negotiations through which defendants agree to cooperate to provide clarity on the evidence in exchange for the revision of charges or a reduction in sentence.

Figure 5.1 shows the sequence of events that follow an offender's path within the criminal justice system after a crime is reported to the police or witnessed by the police. The diagram also summarizes the different options available to authorities to sentence an offender. Two main distinctions are visible in the diagram, processes used for the disposition of felony cases and those used to rule over misdemeanors. Although most students can recognize these processes from the literature explored in introductory criminal justice courses, it is important to remember that jurisdictions vary in the way they follow processes within the criminal justice system. For instance, in some jurisdictions, first time offenders charged with victimless crimes (such as public order offenses, DUIs, or some drug offenses that do not involve distribution of illegal substances), might be able to avoid the formal sentencing process altogether, if recommended to a diversion program (an outcome that we explore in the special issue for this section).

Within the formal process, police officers investigate the crime and file the charges in court. Their work is most often independent from the prosecutor. However, in some cases, police officers do interact with the prosecutor to discuss the evidence available. The police identifies the crime that motivated the arrest. The probable cause (the evidence that the crime occurred) is used to file the complaint against the defendant. Once in court, the prosecutor selects the charges without any input from the judge. Most often, the defense attorney is not involved in the case during this initial phase, although exceptions exist, especially in Federal courts (Wright, 2012).

After the suspect is charged with a crime, the judge typically appoints a probation officer who is in charge of investigating the background of the defendant and completing a *presentence investigation and report*. The probation officer primarily focuses on the defendant's prior criminal involvement, the individual's mental and physical health, his/her family background and employment status. The probation officer does not make recommendations but the

Figure 5.1

What is the sequence of events in the criminal justice system?

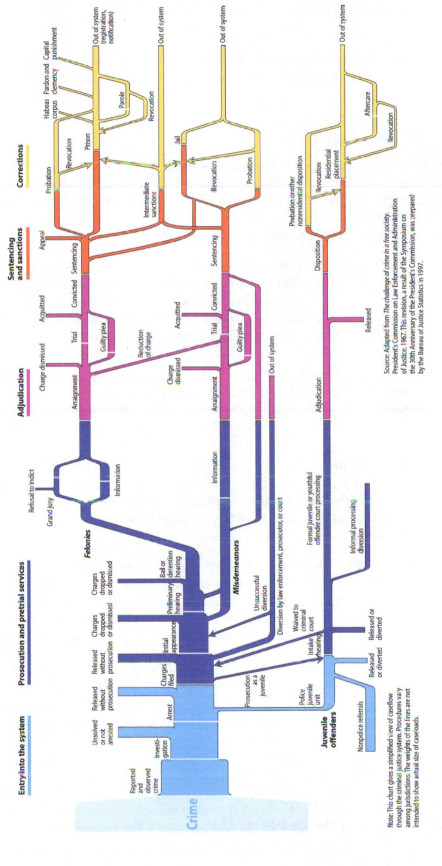

Note: This chart gives a simplified view of caseflow through the criminal justice system. Procedures vary among jurisdictions. The weights of the lines are not intended to show actual size of caseloads.

Source: Adapted from *The challenge of crime in a free society*. President's Commission on Law Enforcement and Administration of Justice. 1967. This revision, a result of the Symposium on the 30th Anniversary of the President's Commission, was prepared by the Bureau of Justice Statistics in 1997.

information provided in the pre-sentence investigation report helps judges identify the most appropriate type of sentence for the defendant (Clear, Reisig, & Cole, 2018).

PLEA BARGAIN

The defense attorney typically enters the case at the initial hearing where the defendant is informed about the charges. Because defendants are most often indigent, the court appoints a public defense attorney to represent the defendant. At this point, the prosecutor and the defense attorney begin the negotiations (Wright, 2012). There are three types of possible concessions: charge bargain, sentence bargain, and fact bargain.

1. *Charge bargain*: the prosecutor might agree to reduce the total number of charges (*horizontal charge bargain*) or to commute the most serious charge to a lesser one (*vertical charge bargain*). In the charge bargain, the judge is typically not involved in the negotiations; however, differences are observed by jurisdiction. In jurisdictions where the judge is included in the negotiations, judges are more likely to accept the plea and expedite the process.

2. *Sentence bargain*: with no reduction of charges, the prosecutor agrees to recommend to the judge a sentence below the maximum penalty for the crime. Sentence bargain is most commonly used in jurisdictions that use mandatory minimum sentences. In this scenario, then, the parties would agree to avoid the application of laws that would result in harsher penalties, especially in federal court for drug and weapon charges.

3. *Fact bargain*: the parties agree on either using certain facts in court or eliminating them from the case to favor the defendant. For instance, because the presence of weapons is in most states an aggravating element, the parties might agree to eliminate the fact from the case and prevent the evidence without discussing the presence of the weapon at the time the "crime" occurred.

The negotiations that occur between the parties are known as "plea bargain" in the American court system. Plea bargain takes place when an agreement is made between the court (prosecutors and judges) and the defendant's attorney to offer the defendant specific concessions in exchange for their admission of guilt or self-conviction. While concessions may vary, they all pertain to the sentence recommended by the prosecutor, the charges filed by the police department, or the punishment identified by the judge. As for the defendant, however, there is no variation. The negotiations are limited to the admission of guilt either real or construed; for instance, no restitution to the victim or resigning from public office can be considered as part of the negotiation (Alschuler, 1979). Sentencing practices that include plea bargain are often seen as controversial in criminal justice and criminology literature (Reiman & Leighton, 2015).

The use of plea negotiations in the U.S. contemporary penal system has become a common practice. Estimates show that between 85% and 95% of criminal cases end up as guilty pleas in which defendants wave their right to trial (Devers, 2011; Harlow, 2001).

The practice of guilty plea as we know it today was not encouraged in the traditional English Common Law (Alschuler, 1979). A principle of Common Law is that the defendant leaves the burden of proving one's guilt to the state. The guilty plea, as a form of self-incrimination, appears to be a distortion of this principle. While confessions were not uncommon in medieval legal practices, there is evidence that the courts used to recommend that the defendant stand trial (Alschuler, 1979). However, legal practices today appear more complex than those of the middle ages (Langbein, 1979). Because the defendant was denied counsel, jurors did not have to pass examination, a necessary process in today's criminal courts. Cross-examinations were quick and the judge had the power to stop a trial at any time or even continue a trial after adjudication, if he did not agree with the jury's decision (Langbein, 1979).

Punishment was harsh in England during the 19th century. Considering that death was the authorized punishment for 220 offenses, one would not be surprised to learn that the courts themselves discouraged the defendant's self-incrimination (Alschuler, 1979). In the United States, plea bargaining was discouraged until the second half of the 19th century, but at the turn of the 20th century, plea bargaining became a common practice. This was in part due to the number of violations that followed the enactment of prohibition laws (Alschuler, 1979). While the guilty plea became more common as a court practice, it was never fully endorsed by the public and the general media.

Plea bargaining is, in its own way, the opposite of litigation. Negotiations occur in private, preventing the public from witnessing justice in action. Concessions to the defendant in exchange of a confession or admission of guilt (whether real or construed) can be seen as coercive because of the threat that maximum penalties will be applied if the route of litigation is chosen. Some scholars even argue that a system that allows for a negotiation of justice tends to undermine the goal of deterrence that is at the core of the U.S. system of punishment and corrections (Smith, 1986).

The fact that many questioned the legality of plea bargaining in the criminal justice system became clear in *Shelton v. United States* (1958), a case that discussed whether prosecutorial promises can be seen as coercive forces altering the principle of voluntary confession in court. However, later decisions of the U.S. Supreme Court have contributed to the acceptance of plea bargaining as a common practice, often necessary to expedite cases within a court system flooded by an overwhelming number of complaints. In the 1970 decision in *Brady v. United States*, the U.S. Supreme Court ruled that plea bargaining is an integral part of criminal law and its administration. More recently, in *Missouri v. Frye* (2012) the U.S. Supreme Court decided that "[…] defense counsel has the duty to communicate formal offers from the prosecution to accept a plea on terms and conditions that may be favorable to the accused" (p. 9). In dissent, some justices saw this decision as a reaffirmation of the existence of a plea bargaining jurisprudence which might or might not have concrete foundations in the defendant's constitutional rights (*Lafler v. Cooper*, 2012).

While constitutional doctrine has established that courts may not subject defendants to punishment for exercising their right to a jury trial (Wright, 2012), the reality today is contradictory. Research findings suggest that sentences imposed in cases of defendants who opted for a jury trial tend to be higher on average than those of defendants accepting plea agreements. While the extent to which defendants are penalized for choosing to go to trial varies depending on the offense and jurisdiction, the mean difference between sentences negotiated through a plea and those decided after a trial is not insignificant (Wright, 2012: 257–258).

SENTENCING MODELS: DETERMINATE AND INDETERMINATE

Since the 1970s, American jurisdictions relied on the *indeterminate* sentencing model which gave judges an unregulated discretion when deciding how to sentence a felon. The only constraint to the judge's discretion was the maximum penalty allowed for each crime. For those who received a prison sentence, the end of their period of incarceration was decided with ample discretion by the parole board. The only limit to such discretion were minimum and maximum terms as defined in State statutory laws (Reitz, 2012). Within the indeterminate sentencing model, two main actors share complete discretion over a case, the judge (front end) who decides upon one's sentence, and the parole board (back end) invested of the power of deciding upon one's release. Because of the framework within which indeterminate sentences are defined, no one (no even the judge) knows how long an offender will stay in prison. *Determinate* sentencing models were introduced in the 1970s to limit the frivolous discretion of many judges around the country (Spohn, 2009). Determinate sentencing models have eliminated the role of the parole board and the possibility of early release as determined by parole regulations (Reitz, 2012).

Within determinate sentencing models, judges assign a term of incarceration that only specifies a range, that is, minimum and maximum period of incarceration. In determinate sentencing models, sentenced offenders complete a substantial portion of the sentence (for instance, with *truth-in sentences,* the proportion set by the state is most commonly 85% of the sentence) minus the time earned for good conduct (Reitz, 2012).

In States that adopted *mandatory minimum sentences*, the judge can define the sentence only within the statutory parameters imposed by the guidelines. The implementation of mandatory minimums dictated that offenders found guilty of specific crimes (e.g., certain drug offences under the War on Drugs legislation) had to serve prison sentences for a number of months/years specified in statutory guidelines.

The "indeterminacy" (or inefficiency) of the indeterminate sentencing model was first condemned by judge Frankel in his 1973 book. It is important to observe that while parole invested the parole board of the task to determine the "moral reformation" of an offender, the reality appeared very different. Because parole board members are appointed via political connections (directly by the Governor of the State), and function with no guidelines behind closed doors, knowing how decisions were made became impossible (Reitz, 2012). Frankel (1973) advocated for a new American Sentencing Commission that would be comprised of sentencing and corrections experts who invested with the difficult task of writing guidelines that would guarantee equity and fairness for all defendants (Spohn, 2009). The best example of sentencing commission is the one most often cited in research papers and textbooks, the Minnesota Sentencing Guidelines Commission created in 1978 (Weisberg, 2012). The Commission was comprised of 11 members; among them were judges, prosecutors, defense attorneys, officials representing parole, probation, and police in addition to members of the general public (including also the victim of a felony crime).

Figure 5.2 shows the grid created by the Minnesota Sentencing Commission to guide judges in determining the appropriate sentence for each specific case.

Other states appointed new commissions to determine new guidelines but not all these efforts actually made a difference. Failures were often the results of judges' rebellion against

Figure 5.2

4.A. Sentencing Guidelines Grid

Presumptive sentence lengths are in months. Italicized numbers within the grid denote the discretionary range within which a court may sentence without the sentence being deemed a departure. Offenders with stayed felony sentences may be subject to local confinement.

SEVERITY LEVEL OF CONVICTION OFFENSE (Example offenses listed in italics)		CRIMINAL HISTORY SCORE						
		0	**1**	**2**	**3**	**4**	**5**	**6 or more**
Murder, 2nd Degree (intentional murder; drive-by-shootings)	**11**	306 *261-367*	326 *278-391*	346 *295-415*	366 *312-439*	386 *329-463*	406 *346-480[2]*	426 *363-480[2]*
Murder, 3rd Degree Murder, 2nd Degree (unintentional murder)	**10**	150 *128-180*	165 *141-198*	180 *153-216*	195 *166-234*	210 *179-252*	225 *192-270*	240 *204-288*
Assault, 1st Degree	**9**	86 *74-103*	98 *84-117*	110 *94-132*	122 *104-146*	134 *114-160*	146 *125-175*	158 *135-189*
Agg. Robbery, 1st Degree; Burglary, 1st Degree (w/ Weapon or Assault)	**8**	48 *41-57*	58 *50-69*	68 *58-81*	78 *67-93*	88 *75-105*	98 *84-117*	108 *92-129*
Felony DWI; Financial Exploitation of a Vulnerable Adult	**7**	36	42	48	54 *46-64*	60 *51-72*	66 *57-79*	72 *62-84[2, 3]*
Assault, 2nd Degree Burglary, 1st Degree (Occupied Dwelling)	**6**	21	27	33	39 *34-46*	45 *39-54*	51 *44-61*	57 *49-68*
Residential Burglary; Simple Robbery	**5**	18	23	28	33 *29-39*	38 *33-45*	43 *37-51*	48 *41-57*
Nonresidential Burglary	**4**	12[1]	15	18	21	24 *21-28*	27 *23-32*	30 *26-36*
Theft Crimes (Over $5,000)	**3**	12[1]	13	15	17	19 *17-22*	21 *18-25*	23 *20-27*
Theft Crimes ($5,000 or less) Check Forgery ($251-$2,500)	**2**	12[1]	12[1]	13	15	17	19	21 *18-25*
Assault, 4th Degree Fleeing a Peace Officer	**1**	12[1]	12[1]	12[1]	13	15	17	19 *17-22*

[1] 12[1]=One year and one day

Presumptive commitment to state imprisonment. First-degree murder has a mandatory life sentence and is excluded from the Guidelines under Minn. Stat. § 609.185. See section 2.E, for policies regarding those sentences controlled by law.

Presumptive stayed sentence; at the discretion of the court, up to one year of confinement and other non-jail sanctions can be imposed as conditions of probation. However, certain offenses in the shaded area of the Grid always carry a presumptive commitment to state prison. See sections 2.C and 2.E.

[2] Minn. Stat. § 244.09 requires that the Guidelines provide a range for sentences that are presumptive commitment to state imprisonment of 15% lower and 20% higher than the fixed duration displayed, provided that the minimum sentence is not less than one year and one day and the maximum sentence is not more than the statutory maximum. See section 2.C.1-2.

[3] The stat. max. for Financial Exploitation of Vulnerable Adult is 240 months; the standard range of 20% higher than the fixed duration applies at CHS 6 or more. (The range is 62-86.)

provisions that would limit their discretion. Over time, the sentencing guidelines have been transformed into a voluntary system that still allows plenty of discretion in the sentencing process, depending on the circumstances of each individual case. A very positive outcome in recent years came from the use of Sentencing Commissions for the collection and analysis of sentencing data (Weisberg, 2012).

PUNISHING OFFENDERS

The U.S. penal system uses a number of sanctions to punish (and in some case rehabilitate) offenders: *incarceration, intermediate sanctions, probation, and death.* Incarceration can involve a period of confinement in jail or prison (either state or federal). In some cases, a defendant may be sentenced to a period of supervision in the community, a probationary period in which the defendant's behavior is closely monitored. While many believe that probation is a lenient form of punishment, the conditions of supervision can be rather strict. Often, probation is accompanied by other intermediate sanctions, such as fines, community service, and participation in mandatory programs (such as substance abuse programs). The most extreme form of punishment (and also the least common) is the death penalty. In the last 10 years, the American death penalty has been subjected to criticism not only within the United States but also internationally. The next sections of the book will focus on all these forms of punishment.

LEARNING EXERCISE

Scenario: On January 2, 2018, Brandon Bennett attended a family gathering in a suburb of Cleveland, Ohio where he had a few drinks before heading home to sleep at 8:30 pm. Because Brandon works for the local hospital as a nurse, he decided to go home early for a good night sleep. On his way home, Brandon was pulled over by the police because he failed to come to a complete stop at one of the intersections in one of the least trafficked neighborhoods near his home. Brandon was frustrated about the situation, but complied with the orders of the police and agreed to complete an alcohol breath test. Because Brandon's test results were above the threshold mandated by the State of Ohio, Brandon was arrested and spent the night in the local jail.

Assignment: Draw a diagram to describe the possible outcome(s) for Brandon in our current U.S. penal system.

BIBLIOGRAPHY

Alschuler, A. W. (1979). Plea bargaining and its history. *Columbia Law Review, 79*(1), 1–43.

Brady v. United States (1970). 397 U.S. 742, 90 S. Ct. 1463, 25 L. Ed. 2d 747.

Chesney-Lind, M., & Mauer, M. (Eds.). (2003). *Invisible punishment: The collateral consequences of mass imprisonment.* New York, NY: The New Press.

Chin, G. J. (2002). Race, the war on drugs, and the collateral consequences of criminal conviction. *Journal of Gender, Race & Justice*, *6*, 253.

Clear, T. R., Reisig, M. D., & Cole, G. F. (2018). *American corrections*. Boston, MA: Cengage Learning.

Devers, L. (2011). Plea and charge bargaining. *Research summary*. Bureau of Justice Assistance, US Department of Justice.

Frankel, M. E. (1973). *Criminal sentences; law without order*. New York, NY: Hill & Wang.

Harlow, C. W. (2001). *Defense counsel in criminal cases*. US Department of Justice, Office of Justice Programs, Bureau of Justice Statistics.

Lafler v. Cooper, (2012). 132 S. Ct. 1376, 566 U.S. 156, 182 L. Ed. 2d 398.

Langbein, J. H. (1979). Understanding the short history of plea bargaining. *Law and Society Review*, 261–272.

Marder, N. S. (2015). Juror bias, voir dire, and the judge-jury relationship.

Missouri v. Frye, (2012). 132 S. Ct. 1399, 566 U.S. 134, 182 L. Ed. 2d 379.

Petersilia, J., & Reitz, K. R. (2012). Introduction sentencing and corrections: Overlapping and inseparable subjects. In Petersilia, J., & Reitz, K. R. (Eds.), *The Oxford Handbook of Sentencing & Corrections* (pp. 3–20). New York, NY: Oxford University Press.

Pinard, M. (2006). An integrated perspective on the collateral consequences of criminal convictions and reentry issues faced by formerly incarcerated individuals. *Boston University Law Review*, *86*, 623.

Reiman, J., & Leighton, P. (2015). *The rich get richer and the poor get prison: Ideology, class, and criminal justice*. New York, NY: Routledge.

Reitz, K. R. (2012). The "traditional" indeterminate sentencing model. In J. Petersilia, & K. R. Reitz (Eds.), *The Oxford Handbook of Sentencing & Corrections* (pp. 270–298). New York, NY: Oxford University Press.

Shelton v. United States (1958). 356 U.S. 26, 78 S. Ct. 563, 2 L. Ed. 2d 579.

Smith, D. A. (1986). The plea bargaining controversy. *The Journal of Criminal Law and Criminology (1973–)*, *77*(3), 949–968.

Spohn, C. (2009). *How do judges decide? The search for fairness and justice in punishment*. Thousand Oaks, CA: Sage.

Travis, J. (2002). Invisible punishment: An instrument of social exclusion.

Weisberg, R. (2012). The sentencing commission model, 1970s to present. In J. Petersilia, & K. R. Reitz (Eds.), *The Oxford Handbook of Sentencing & Corrections* (pp. 299–316). New York, NY: Oxford University Press.

Wright, R. F. (2012). Charging and plea bargaining as forms of sentencing discretion. In J. Petersilia, & K. R. Reitz (Eds.), *The Oxford Handbook of Sentencing & Corrections* (pp. 247–269). New York, NY: Oxford University Press.

Problem-Solving Courts

Following an expansion of the criminal justice system and the consequential overcrowding of jails and prisons, problem-solving courts were established in the United States in the late 1980s (Nolan, 2012; Rottman & Casey, 1999).

The first problem-solving court was created in Miami by Judge Goldstein in 1989 (Nolan, 2003, 2012). The idea of a problem-solving court was to tackle the problem at the core of the criminal behavior while keeping the offender out of the criminal justice system. The concept of problem-solving court is based on the philosophy of therapeutic jurisprudence which attempts to correct criminal behavior through treatment instead of involving the offender in the traditional system of punishment. Problem-solving courts in the United States are also called *diversion programs* in that they offer solution outside the formal process of sentencing and corrections (Stefan & Winick, 2005). By providing opportunities for rehabilitation, problem-solving courts tend to reduce the number of criminal records. Offenders who successfully complete diversion programs will have their criminal cases eliminated from the court records.

By agreeing to participate in a diversion program, the defendant also agrees to stay out of trouble while complying with the requirements of the problem-solving court. The nature of the "treatment" assigned by the judge often depends on the type of problem-solving court disciplining the case. There are many different types of problem-solving courts in the United States. While drugs courts were the first problem-solving courts to be established, today problem-solving courts include domestic violence courts, veteran courts, homeless courts, community courts, DUI courts, gambling courts, mental health courts, and reentry courts (Nolan, 2012).

BIBLIOGRAPHY

Nolan Jr, J. L. (2003). Redefining criminal courts: Problem-solving and the meaning of justice. *American Criminal Law Review*, *40*, 1541–1565.

Nolan Jr, J. L. (2012). Problem-solving courts: An international comparison. In J. Petersilia, & K. R. Reitz (Eds.), *The Oxford Handbook of Sentencing & Corrections*. New York, NY: Oxford University Press.

Rottman, D., & Casey, P. (1999). Therapeutic jurisprudence and the emergence of problem-solving courts. *National Institute of Justice Journal*, *240*, 12–19.

Stefan, S., & Winick, B. J. (2005). A dialogue on mental health courts. *Psychology, Public Policy, and Law*, *11*(4), 507–526.

Section III

Corrections in the Community

A small house with a red roof is wrapped in metal chain. The concept of security, legality, arrest. 3D rendering.

© cherezoff/Shutterstock.com

CHAPTER 6

Overview of Community Corrections

INTRODUCTION

Section II focused entirely on Sentencing, the complex process employed by the court to determine the appropriate sanction to punish and rehabilitate an offender. This section (and the next sections of the book) focuses on Corrections. Sentencing and Corrections are the two sides of the modern system of punishment; they are intertwined.

"Community corrections" is the term used to refer to practices of punishment and rehabilitation that replace incarceration. In criminology and criminal justice books, the term community corrections is often used in opposition to "institutional corrections" which refers to the various sanctions that involve the confinement of offenders (jails, prisons). The most common forms of sanctions in the community are probation and parole. However, as technology allows for a more sophisticated approach to community supervision, new forms of intermediate sanctions become available (Taxman, 2012). The War on Drugs caused an explosion of cases that required the supervision of offenders in the community. The caseload of probation officers grew rapidly, reaching a 1:100 ratio (number of officers per number of offenders) very fast (Taxman, 2012). Within this scenario, scholars proposed that additional forms of community supervision be added to allow for the processing of a growing number of offenders sentenced to probation (Morris & Tonry, 1991).

At present, the U.S. criminal justice system offers an array of community-based programs. For instance, problem-solving courts (featured in the special issue for Section II of this book) are becoming a large component of the community-based correctional system and represent a form of diversion program often used with first time offenders. States vary in the number and type of community-based programs offered and in the way supervision takes place within these programs (Taxman, 2012). In addition, community service, house arrest with electronic monitoring, intense supervision programs (ISPs), and monetary fines are among the most utilized programs throughout the nation (Welch, 2013). Multiple community-based programs are sometimes used for the same offender. This choice often stems from the need to address the diverse set of correctional goals of punishment, rehabilitation, restitution, incapacitation, and rehabilitation all at once. Decisions are usually finalized based on the offender's needs and risk of reoffending. For instance, consider the case of an offender charged for driving under the influence (DUI). This individual might be placed on probation within an intensive supervision program while being court mandated to attend a substance abuse or alcohol abuse recovery program (Welch, 2013).

Community-based programs are often seen as helpful alternatives to incarceration as they appear to contain the problem of jail and prison overcrowding. In addition, because community-based programs do not require the housing of offenders (confinement), they are deemed as cost-effective (Welch, 2013). While the public often perceives community corrections to be a lenient alternative to incarceration ("a slap on the wrist"), critics have for long time argued that community corrections can be even more invasive than institutional corrections while also adding costs and responsibilities that tend to hinder an offender's ability to comply with the agreement stipulated with the court (Teague, 2011). Foucault had a very critical perspective on the use community-based sanctions as alternatives to incarceration. According to Foucault (1977), the mechanisms arranged to control individuals in the community were simply different ways to achieve the same results through surveillance and deprivation outside the walls.

Bureau of Justice Statistics' estimates show that, by December 2015, there were 4,650,900 people under community supervision. Among them, 4,518,100 (1,814 per 100,000 residents) were under State supervision while the remaining 132,800 (53 per 100,000 residents) were under Federal supervision (Kaeble & Bonczar, 2016). These figures indicate that at the end of 2015, roughly 1 every 53 adults was under some form of community supervision, an improvement from the 1 every 45 adults estimates recorded during the early 2000s (Herberman & Bonczar, 2014). As these numbers suggest, community corrections today is an important component of the U.S. criminal justice system as is responsible for the supervision, punishment, and rehabilitation of the largest share of the offender population. However, its mission cannot be studied as a separate entity; community corrections is an integral part of corrections, in general, and its existence can only be understood in association with the history of institutional corrections. Community-based corrections has evolved side-by-side the American prison system (Wodahl & Garland, 2009).

EVOLUTION OF COMMUNITY-BASED CORRECTIONS

The Enlightenment changed the way western societies viewed punishment. Guided by the work of Cesare Beccaria, American penal reformers embraced the idea that punishment must fit the crime and corporal punishment and the death penalty should be used only in extreme cases (Rothman, 1971). In the 18th century, incarceration appeared as a more humane form of punishment than the use of torture and physical punishment that characterized medieval European societies (Newman, 1985). By adjusting the length of incarceration, the State would be able to guarantee the principle of proportionality (Rothman, 1971). Penal reformers of the 18th century believed that incarceration would allow to maintain a goal of deterrence within a growing system of punishment and corrections (Wodahl & Garland, 2009). However, by the turn of the 19th century, it was apparent that the principle of deterrence that the prison represented did not actually work. Prisons were mismanaged and the rehabilitative ideal proved very difficult to achieve (Wodahl & Garland, 2009). In fact, critics of the prison system denounced the harsh impact that confinement had on the offenders. Convicted offenders who spent time in prison were hardened by the experience, proving that confinement did not help rehabilitate offenders but rather contributed to the problem of recidivism (Foucault, 1977). Although it became evident that prisons did not work to rehabilitate offenders, the expansion of the prison system continued well into the first decade of the 21st century (Zimring, 2010).

The idea of community-based supervision did not fully develop in its modern form until the mid-19th century, right when the inability of the prison system to reform offenders became accepted as a reality (Wodahl & Garland, 2009). With high rates of re-offending, and the inhumane conditions within prisons around the nation, creating alternatives to incarceration became a priority (Wodahl & Garland, 2009).

Probation and parole were the first two forms of community-based corrections implemented in the United States in the 19th century. While the origins of both probation and parole can be traced back to correctional practices used in Europe during the 1800s, probation developed to be "an American innovation" (Wodahl & Garland, 2009: 865). The dissatisfaction with the prison as an institution of punishment and rehabilitation continued to grow, and community-based corrections developed to complement the mission of the existing institutions of corrections. However, just as much as the prison never embodied the ideal of rehabilitation, probation and parole also failed to provide the support that offenders placed under supervision needed (Wodahl & Garland, 2009). The main reason explaining the inadequacy of both prisons and community-based corrections throughout the 1900s was their inability to reproduce the actual intent of the penal reformers (Wodahl & Garland, 2009). Recruitment of qualified personnel was a challenge because these occupations did not pay enough to attract individuals with formal education. In addition, the heavy caseload and the personnel's lack of training limited the opportunity to have a positive influence on offenders (Wodahl & Garland, 2009). Despite the evidence that community-based corrections did not achieve the goal of rehabilitation that was in the mind of the penal reformers of the 19th century, these alternatives to incarceration continued to receive support. The popularity of community corrections was not due to its effectiveness but to the opportunity to support the interests of various groups within the criminal justice system. For instance, probation allowed attorneys to persuade their clients to accept a guilty plea while also providing judges with an alternative for punishment. Parole helped prison administrators with the containment of disciplinary problems, as early release was often considered a form of reward for well-behaved inmates (Rothman, 2002; Wodahl & Garland, 2009). In addition, the presence of a parole board to make decisions for the release of inmates with records of good behavior would lift some of the judge's responsibility for any crime committed by an offender released on parole (Rothman, 2002). There was also hope that community-based corrections would help reform offenders at a time when the dissatisfaction with institutional corrections became more intense during the 1960s, as the conditions of penal institutions continued to deteriorate (Wodahl & Garland, 2009). While community corrections alternatives were highly criticized because of the high rates of recidivism, their use continued to grow throughout the 20th century because they offered cheaper alternatives to confinement (Wodahl & Garland, 2009).

Today, community corrections receive support from both progressives and conservatives. Progressives believe that a community-based supervision is more humane than confinement in prison facilities. Conservatives believe that the new technology employed to monitor offenders in the community will help keep the communities safe while also reducing the costs of punishment (Wodahl & Garland, 2009). However, technology also allows for an oppressive type of surveillance in that it can enter a person's home via the use of an electronic device attached to the offender's body (like in the case of an ankle bracelet). Schenwar (2014) condemns the use of technology for surveillance purposes as a constant attack to the individual's constitutional rights in that it allows for continuous unjustified searches. What is concerning is that the public has accepted the normalization of a total exercise of social control over civilians (Schenwar, 2014).

LEARNING EXERCISES

For discussion:

- What are the principles and ideals behind community-based corrections?
- Are community corrections alternatives less severe forms of punishment? Explain.
- What would be some innovations that would make community corrections better alternatives to incarceration?

BIBLIOGRAPHY

Foucault, M. (1977). *Discipline and punish* (A. Sheridan, trans.). New York: Pantheon.

Herberman, E. J. & Bonczar, T. (2014). *Probation & Parole in the United States, 2013*. Washington, DC: U.S. Department of Justice, Bureau of Justice Statistics. NCJ, 248029.

Kaeble, D., Maruschak, L., & Bonczar, T. (2015). *Probation and Parole in the United States, 2014*. Washington, DC: U.S. Department of Justice, Bureau of Justice Statistics. NCJ 250230.

Morris, N., & Tonry, M. (1991). *Between prison and probation: Intermediate punishments in a rational sentencing system*. New York, NY: Oxford University Press.

Newman, G. R. (1985). *The punishment response*. Albany, NY: Transaction publishers.

Rothman, D. J. (1971). *The discovery of the asylum*. Albany, NY: Transaction Publishers.

Rothman, D. J. (2002). *Conscience and convenience: The asylum and its alternatives in progressive America*. New York, NY: Routledge.

Schenwar, M. (2014). *Locked down, locked out: Why prison doesn't work and how we can do better*. San Francisco, CA: Berrett-Koehler Publishers.

Taxman, F. S. (2012). Probation, intermediate sanctions, and community-based corrections. In J. Petersilia, & K. R. Reitz (Eds.), *The Oxford handbook of sentencing and corrections* (pp. 363–385). New York, NY: Oxford University Press.

Teague, M. (2011). Probation in America: Armed, private and unaffordable? *Probation Journal, 58*(4), 317–332.

Welch, M. (2013). *Corrections: A critical approach* (3rd ed.), New York, NY: Routledge.

Wodahl, E. J., & Garland, B. (2009). The evolution of community corrections. *The Prison Journal, 89*(1_suppl), 81S–104S.

Zimring, F. E. (2010). The scale of imprisonment in the United States: Twentieth century patterns and twenty-first century prospects. *The Journal of Criminal Law and Criminology (1973–), 100*(3), 1225–1246.

CHAPTER 7

Probation

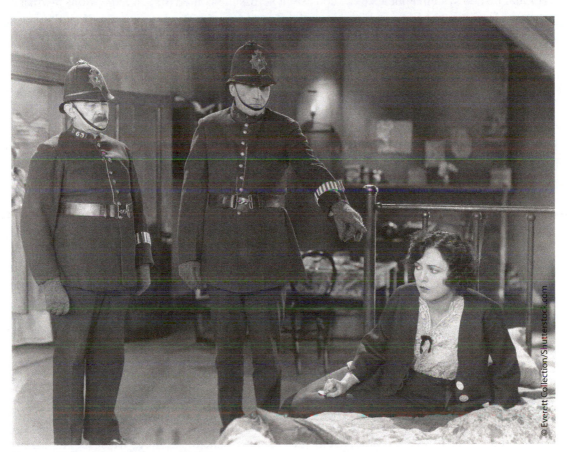

House arrest

LEARNING OBJECTIVES

- Identify the key elements of probation
- Discuss the challenges associated with offenders completing a probation sentence in the community
- Describe pros and cons of probation
- Reflect on the need for change in the use of probation

INTRODUCTION

The term "probation" comes from the Latin *probation* which means "test or approval" (Welch, 2013: 439). The Bureau of Justice Statistics defines probation as "a court-ordered period of correctional supervision in the community, generally as an alternative to incarceration" (Herberman & Bonczar, 2014: 2). This definition provides a clear idea of what probation actually is, the ideology behind it, and its application. While jurisdictions may vary in the way they experiment probation for particular cases of offenders, the use of probation in the adult criminal justice system appears to be consistent across the United States. Exceptions are made when probation is used in combination with other sentences. The Bureau of Justice Statistics specifies that "[i]n some cases, probation can be a combined sentence of incarceration followed by a period of community supervision" (Herberman & Bonczar, 2014: 2).

THE CURRENT SCENARIO

At the end of 2013, there were 4.7 million adults under community corrections supervision in the United States; among them, 82% were under probation supervision (Herberman & Bonczar, 2014). The adult probation population has declined consistently throughout the 2005 to 2015 period, a decrease from 1,864 per 100,000 residents to 1,522 per 100,000 U.S. residents. The percentage of offenders admitted to a correctional facility because of a violation of the terms of probation also fell significantly during the last 10 years moving from a 25% rate in 2005 to 14% rate in 2015 (Kaeble & Bonczar, 2016). With a total adult probation population of 481,339 (or 5,570 per 100,000 residents), the state of Georgia is the state with the largest concentration of adults under the supervision of probation departments (Kaeble & Bonczar, 2016). This appears to be a major improvement from the situation reported in 2013, when Georgia had 515,896 adults on probation, that is 6,829 probationers every 100,000 residents (Herberman & Bonczar, 2013).

DOES PROBATION WORK?

Scholars discussed the benefits probation might have not just for the individual offender but for the community as well when compared to other criminal sanctions (Stohr, Walsh, & Hemmens, 2009). While some "at risk" offenders cannot make it on probation because of their inability to adapt to the conditions imposed by the court (Stohr, Walsh, & Hemmens, 2009), the majority of offenders placed on probation will complete a sentence in the community and never enter the prison (Petersilia, 1985). Even when probation violations occur, research shows that the majority of infractions are actually minor technical violations of probation agreements. Risk factors, such as a history of drug abuse, low educational attainment, and unemployment tend to be strong predictors of probation violations (Gray, Fields, & Maxwell, 2001).

In many ways, the community benefits from re-directing the offender from a sentence of incarceration to a period of community supervision in that probation tends to save communities significant amounts of money. Overall, the costs associated with the supervision of an individual offender on probation are low compared to the costs of incarceration. Estimates show that keeping an offender on probation for a year can be 20 times cheaper than placing the same offender in a correctional facility (Stohr, Walsh, & Hemmens, 2009). In addition, in some jurisdictions, probation fees are part of the responsibility of the offender, making probation a more efficient system of corrections than other forms of supervision (Stohr, Walsh, & Hemmens, 2009). Furthermore, by not removing offenders from their homes, the community benefits from avoiding the disruption that incarceration causes when offenders are taken away from their families. When offenders on probation can also keep their jobs, criminal justice operations become more manageable. This is not to say that probation is easier than other criminal sentences, but in some way, it might help prevent many of the disruptions that incarceration causes to individuals and communities.

An area of research that is underdeveloped pertains to the impact that probation supervision may have on the health of probation officers. Empirical findings from extant studies vary significantly based on the instruments utilized to measure work-related stress and its consequences. The overall evidence, however, is that probation officers are among the most stressed out people at the job (Whitehead & Lindquist, 1985). This might be due to the high level of responsibilities they face as they attempt to prevent further harm to the community. Moreover, many offenders are difficult to manage because of mental health problems, substance abuse, or inability to maintain employment (Slate, Wells, & Johnson, 2003). It is possible that additional costs need to be added to the existing estimates mentioned earlier when discussing the costs of managing the probation population. The costs associated to employees' sick leaves, turnover due to burnout, and the continuous training of new employees that follows should also be taken into consideration.

HISTORY OF PROBATION

The use of probation in the United States came from the English Common law practice of suspending an offender's sentence as an opportunity for redemption under the agreement to demonstrate good behavior. The pioneer of probation is known as John Augustus, a Boston bootmaker and a merchant often considered as a "true savior" (Welch, 2013). In the 1840s, Augustus voiced his concerns over the conditions of the jails and realized that a large number of those confined were indigent people who happened to be alcoholics. As a compassionate individual, Augustus observed that detention actually worsened the situation. He then began to advocate for a new criminal justice model that would provide support for first time offenders by placing them under community supervision as they received the treatment they needed. Most importantly, Augustus believed that within this new criminal justice concept, offenders could continue to work and maintain their position in the community (Taxman, 2012). Augustus' ideas were well received not only in Boston but throughout the state of Massachusetts and by 1957 his punishment model was implemented by all the states. The initial community corrections' model focused on a social work approach that would target directly the offender's mental health problems, alcoholism, and other social needs (Taxman, 2012).

In 1932, in *Burn v. United States*, the U.S. Supreme Court ruled that "probation is not a privilege and cannot be demanded as a right." Perhaps the most official recognition of probation as a form of sanction came in the 1943. In *Roberts v. United States, the U.S. Supreme*

Court ruled that "probation is to be used to provide an individualized program offering a young or unhardened offender an opportunity to rehabilitate himself without institutional confinement under the tutelage of a probation officer" (Welch, 2013: 440).

In Section II, an overview of the sentencing process clarified how an individual might be placed on probation or incarceration. Below, a more detailed description of the process is provided.

PRESENTENCE INVESTIGATION AND REPORT

The *Presentence Investigation and Report* (PSI) constitutes a thorough examination of the defendant's risk and needs conducted to identify the most appropriate sentence (punishment and rehabilitation). The PSI involves the interviews of people with whom the defendant has regular contacts and seeks to understand the personality of the individual in addition to an explanation for the circumstances that led to the offense. Official records of the defendant's whereabouts are also analyzed (medical records, school, employment, and court records) (Mays & Winfree, 2014).

Depending on the jurisdiction, the PSI may actually be the first document prepared within the court and represent the most relevant document to inform the prosecutor's decision to offer a plea agreement. Courts often rely on both the PSI and the results of risk and needs assessments (actuarial measures) to identify the level of supervision needed, the additional community-based programs, and the length of the sentence as well (Mays & Winfree, 2014).

PROBATION SUPERVISION

Probation supervision can be administrative, minimum supervision, medium supervision, or intensive supervision (Mays & Winfree, 2014; Pearson, 1988). *Administrative supervision* is most often assigned to offenders who pose no risk to the community. Contacts with the assigned supervisors (probation officers) are usually minimal. Similarly, *minimum supervision* refers to supervision assigned to low-profile offenders, most often misdemeanants or low-level property felons. A defendant placed on minimum supervision usually has only monthly visitations with a supervisor, most often via phone or mail. *Medium supervision* is usually assigned to offenders who have a significant criminal history but do not present a threat to public safety at the time of the sentence. This type of supervision requires that the defendant meets at least once per month with the probation officer. In addition, the officer can make occasional visits to the offender's residence or place of employment. *Intensive supervision* is usually assigned to probationers who have a history of aggression and violent behavior. Intensive supervision programs constitute specific intermediate sanctions managed by probation administrators (Mays & Winfree, 2014). A discussion of intensive supervision and other intermediate sanctions is provided in Chapter 8.

Table 7.1 focuses on the most commonly imposed conditions of probation.

Table 7.1 General conditions of probation

1. Throughout the period of supervision, the probationer must maintain a close communication with the assigned probation officer both verbally and in writing (or in any other form as agreed on).
2. In the event that the probationer is arrested for any violation of the law, the probationer must immediately contact the probation officer assigned.
3. Abusing alcohol or drugs is not allowed during the period of probation.
4. Accessing firearms is not allowed during the period of probation.
5. For a probationer who is employed, any change in employment must be immediately reported to the probation officer.
6. Any change of address (or living conditions) must be notified to the probation officer.
7. Mobility is reduced during probation; any travel outside the assigned jurisdiction must be approved by the probation officer.
8. Applying for a driver's license is not allowed without the approval of the probation officer.
9. During the period of probation, the probationer is not allowed to hang out with delinquent peers.
10. The probationer cannot apply for a marriage license without the probation officer's approval.

Source: Adapted from Mays & Winfree (2014: 85).

THE REVOCATION OF PROBATION

Because probation is a privilege and not a right, probation can be revoked when the offender does not respect the conditions of the probation agreement; such violations are referred to as *technical violations of probation*. Jurisdictions around the United States use a standardized process to rule over technical violations of probation. In two U.S. Supreme Court decisions, *Mempa v. Rhay* (1967) and *Gagnon v. Scarpelli* (1973), the court ruled that probationers receive formal notice of the charges following technical violations of probation and the specific date of the hearing. The *preliminary hearing* is the first step in the process. The probationer might decide to accept a guilty plea and be either imprisoned or given a warning that the condition of probation might be tightened. However, in the event that the probationer pleas not guilty, the process of revocation of probation begins.

Although probation is a privilege, and as a privilege it can be revoked for technical violations, the defendant still has the right to due process. In other words, the defendant must be given the opportunity to testify and present witnesses. However, the court can apply the preponderance of evidence standard that is used in civil cases for the case disposal. In addition, evidence from hearsay can be allowed in court in cases of violation of probation agreements (hearsay would not be allowed in criminal trials). If after the revocation hearing the judge finds the defendant guilty, the probationer might be incarcerated or given another probation sentence, often under stricter conditions (Mays & Winfree, 2014).

LEARNING EXERCISE

Write a case study representing an offender placed on probation. Make sure to provide all the details of the offense and the process through which the level of supervision is identified. Follow the information provided in this chapter to design a possible scenario.

BIBLIOGRAPHY

Burns v. United States (1932). 287 U.S. 216, 53 S. Ct. 154, 77 L. Ed. 266.

Gray, M. K., Fields, M., & Maxwell, S. R. (2001). Examining probation violations: Who, what, and when. *Crime & Delinquency*, *47*(4), 537–557.

Herberman, E. J. & Bonczar, T. (2014). *Probation & Parole in the United States, 2013*. Washington, DC: U.S. Department of Justice, Bureau of Justice Statistics. NCJ, 248029.

Kaeble, D., Maruschak, L., & Bonczar, T. (2015). *Probation and Parole in the United States, 2014*. Washington, DC: U.S. Department of Justice, Bureau of Justice Statistics. NCJ 250230.

Mays, G. L., & Winfree Jr, L. T. (2014). *Essentials of corrections*. Malden, MA: Wiley Blackwell.

Pearson, F. S. (1988). Evaluation of New Jersey's intensive supervision program. *Crime & Delinquency*, *34*(4), 437–448.

Petersilia, J. (1985). Community supervision: Trends and critical issues. *Crime & Delinquency*, *31*(3), 339–347.

Roberts v. United States (1943) 320 U.S. 264, 64 S. Ct. 113, 88 L. Ed. 41.

Slate, R. N., Wells, T. L., & Johnson, W. W. (2003). Opening the manager's Door: State probation officer stress and perceptions of participation in workplace decision making. *Crime & Delinquency*, *49*(4), 519–541.

Stohr, M., Walsh, A., & Hemmens, C. (2009). *Corrections: A text/reader* (Vol. 3). Thousand Oaks, CA: Sage.

Taxman, F. S. (2012). Probation, intermediate sanctions, and community-based corrections. In J. Petersilia, & K. R. Reitz (Eds.), *The Oxford handbook of sentencing and corrections* (pp. 363–385). New York, NY: Oxford University Press.

Welch, M. (2013). *Corrections: A critical approach* (3rd ed.), New York, NY: Routledge.

Whitehead, J., & Lindquist, C. (1985). Job stress and burnout among probation/parole officers: Perceptions and causal factors. *International Journal of Offender Therapy and Comparative Criminology*, *29*(2), 109–119.

CHAPTER 8

Other Programs in the Community

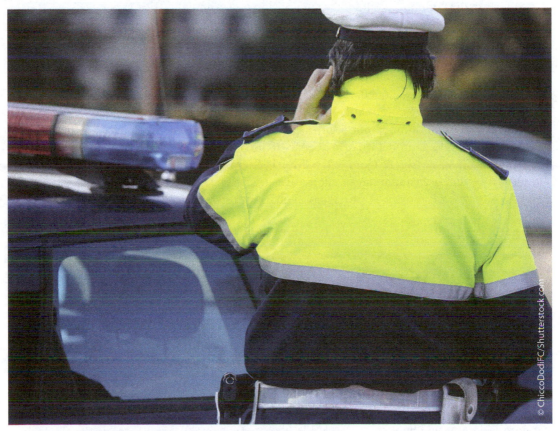

Policeman in a fluorescent jacket while talking on the phone with his superior to handle an emergency

LEARNING OBJECTIVES

- Describe the various alternatives to incarceration and probation available in the U.S. criminal justice system
- Discuss the pros and cons of the different intermediate sanctions
- Provide alternatives for the future of the U.S. criminal justice system

INTRODUCTION

The rapid growth in incarceration rates experienced in the United States during the years between 1990 and 2010 led to an expansion of correctional programs that allow offenders to complete a sentence in the community. These sanctions are often considered as more humane forms of punishment when compared to incarceration in that they allow convicted offenders to continue living in their homes, maintain employment, and preserve family relationships. In addition, community-based corrections allow for the containment of the soaring costs of incarceration. As Clear and collaborators point out, the United States allocates more than $60 billion dollars to corrections every year, of which 90% goes to prisons and jails for the incarceration of offenders. Estimates indicate that a year spent behind bars can be up to 50 times more expensive than a year in the community under the supervision of a criminal justice agency (Clear, Reisig, & Cole, 2016). In addition to the high costs associated with incarceration, confinement in jails or prison facilities has proven ineffective. Cullen, Jonson, and Nagin (2011) found that when empirical measures are rigorously employed to estimate the effect of incarceration, the results unequivocally lead to conclude that supervision in the community tends to show lower recidivism rates. As Clear et al. stated, "[p]erhaps going to prison makes people less likely to obey the law, or staying in the community makes adjustment to law-abiding life easier" (2016: 228).

While incarceration does not seem to be the right choice in many cases, especially for non-violent offenders, probation also appears to be used excessively in the U.S. criminal justice system (Clear, Reisig, & Cole, 2016; Morris & Tonry, 1991). Today, the American criminal justice system uses a number of alternatives (also referred to as "intermediate sanctions") that allow for the placement of offenders in different programs based on the individual's risk and needs.

INTERMEDIATE SANCTIONS

A number of intermediate sanctions are used in the U.S. criminal justice system. Clear et al. (2016) group intermediate sanctions by the agency that is charge of their administration: (1) the judiciary, (2) the probation department, and (3) the department of corrections. Under the administration of the judiciary are pre-trial diversion, fines, forfeiture, and community service and restitution. To these, Welch (2011) adds pre-trial release programs and dispute resolution programs. Under the administration of probation departments are day reporting centers, intensive supervision programs, home confinement, and electronic monitoring. Finally, shock incarceration programs and boot camps are under the supervision of corrections' departments.

Pre-trial diversion is an alternative to prosecution that targets first time offenders charged with minor violations of criminal law. The program is voluntary and an individual identified by the judiciary as eligible for the program has the right to decline participation in the diversion program. Pre-trial diversion was first created in 1947 as a Federal program to allow juveniles charged with a delinquent act to avoid prosecution (Ulrich, 2002). The program was later expanded to offer the possibility to address the causes behind the arrest.

The main objective of diversion programs is to impact an offender's trajectory by attempting to remove an individual's specific needs that might have led to the offense in the first place. An important element of pre-trial diversion is that the accused must receive counsel prior to making a decision to participate in the program (Ulrich, 2002). Perhaps the most beneficial aspect of pre-trial diversion is that upon completion of the program, all the charges are dropped and no record follows the defendant for life, a significant difference from other alternative sanctions. Programs identified as components of the pre-trial diversion vary depending on the individual's needs. Often counseling and community services are used as a combination of punishment and rehabilitation. However, if the defendant fails to comply with the requirements of the program, the prosecution of the case resumes (Welch, 2011).

Pre-trial release is an alternative to jail detention for individuals charged with a crime while awaiting disposal of the case. For defendants who are non-violent and pose no risk to the community, the opportunity to continue to work and remain connected to their families are great advantages (Welch, 2011). Bureau of Justice Statistics' estimates (Cohen, 2012) show that among all the pre-trial cases in Federal district courts filed between 2008 and 2010, property crime offenders were those more likely to be released while illegal immigrants were the least likely to be released. With the Bail Reform Act of 1966, Congress mandated that defendants charged with noncapital offenses in federal courts be granted pre-trial release either via an unsecured bond option or on their own recognizance. The act was later modified in 1984 to include additional cases of defendants that would endanger the community or abscond, failing to appear in court for trial (Cohen, 2012).

Evidence exists that race becomes a deterministic factor in the decision to release a defendant pre-trial. Bureau of Justice Statistics data show that 65% of White defendants, 43% of Blacks/African Americans, 54% of Native Americans/Alaskan Natives, 66% of Asian/Pacific Islander defendants, and only 20% of Hispanics/Latinos were granted pre-trial release between 2008 and 2010 (Cohen, 2012).

Fines are often added to other intermediate sanctions or to a sentence of probation, but only rarely a defendant is punished solely through fines. Many courts around the country, however, struggle to collect the fines imposed on offenders. Most offenders in the United States are indigent and struggle with meaningful and long-term employment. This also may contribute to the disparities that occur in the criminal justice system because affluent defendants are able to pay their fines and move on with their lives while indigent defendants will continue to owe money to the court (Clear, Reisig, & Cole, 2016).

Another monetary penalty among the intermediate sanctions is *restitution*, a payment the defendant is ordered to make directly to the victim or to the "victim fund" for other crime victims. In several states restitution is a component of Victim-Offender Reconciliation Programs (VORPs) through which courts mediate agreements between parties that result in the victim's compensation for a financial, physical, or emotional loss (Clear, Reisig, & Cole, 2016; Welch, 2011).

Forfeiture is a penalty often imposed pre-trial by agencies of the criminal justice system targeting the defendant's property that is believed to be involved in a criminal operation. While forfeiture makes sense within the purpose of the 1970 Racketeer Influenced and Corrupt Organizations Act (RICO) that targeted criminal organizations, scholars argue that confiscating one's property prior to a judicial hearing might become a violation of civil rights (Clear, Reisig, & Cole, 2016). In 1993, in *Austin v. United States*, the U.S. Supreme Court ruled that the eighth amendment also applies to forfeiture cases.

Community service is another type of intermediate sanction that is administered by the judiciary. Community service imposes the completion of a pre-determined number of hours of service to the community, such as street cleaning, hospital volunteering, preparation of dilapidated buildings for restoration, service in nursing homes, etc. The roots of community service can be traced back to ancient civilizations (Bazemore, 1998; Schafer, 1970; Welch, 2011). In modern societies, community service is often used to support those low-income offenders who cannot afford to pay fines (Welch, 2011).

As Welch (2011) points out, courts often provide dispute resolution or conflict resolution programs that allow the parties to reach an agreement. This form of resolution can involve also victims who do not have any personal relationship with the defendant. Conflict can cause serious disruptions to communities and solving disputes outside the court system might prove a more effective solution (O'Leary & Newman, 1970).

In some states, courts can also mandate defendants to enroll in treatment programs. In such cases, defendants are also responsible for the program's enrollment fees. Examples of this are Batterer Intervention Programs (BIPs). States vary in the way they regulate services offered by providers outside the criminal justice system (Pepin, Hoss, & Penn, 2015). In the state of Indiana, for instance, service providers must be certified by the Indiana Coalition Against Domestic Violence (ICADV) and provide services that are in conformity with the state standards for batterer intervention programs.

Intermediate sanctions administered by probation departments usually target more serious cases. When an individual placed on probation appears to be "at-risk" for re-offending, probation administrators can assign the defendant to specific programs that require participation in daily activities meant to either monitor or rehabilitate offenders. In most cases, the purpose of programs like day reporting, half-way houses, or work release programs is to both monitor and rehabilitate offenders who are at high risk for relapse (especially substance abuse offenders) or recidivism. The idea behind *work release* programs and *half-way houses* is to partially detain offenders while also providing them with the opportunity to work and attend specialized programs both within the facility and outside in the community. Both programs focus on a gradual release of offenders back into the communities while providing the much needed support many offenders need before they are ready to be re-integrated into society (Welch, 2011).

Intensive supervision programs (ISPs) are used is addition to probation sentences and they are meant to guarantee a higher level of supervision for offenders sentenced for serious crimes (Stohr, Walsh, & Hemmens, 2009). ISPs require that defendants maintain frequent contacts with the assigned supervisors. Additional services are often required for serious offenders who are also substance abusers. In this case, services might include substance abuse treatment, the use of breathalyzers, urinalysis, and un-announced searches. While some evidence exists that ISPs reduce the risk of re-arrest among defendants, the constant supervision place ISPs defendants at a higher risk for technical violations (Clear, Reisig, & Cole, 2016).

Through *home confinement* (or house arrest) a defendant's movement can be completely or partially restricted. For instance, initially the defendant might be required to spend the entire time at home and have restricted visitations, most often limited to close family members. After a certain number of days, the defendant might be allowed to attend school or return to work, but his/her movements might be monitored through the use of an electronic devise (*electronic monitoring*). While electronic monitoring sanctions are welcome because they allow a defendant to avoid incarceration, they are often seen as invasive and extremely expensive (Clear, Reisig, & Cole, 2016; Schenwar, 2014).

An offender sentenced to a period of probation supervision may also be sentenced to a period of *shock incarceration,* in a jail or prison (Stohr, Walsh, & Hemmens, 2009). The period of incarceration is typically no longer than 90 days. The purpose of shock incarceration is to remind the defendant of the harsh reality of the prison experience with the expectation that he/she would want to avoid long-term confinement at all costs. Critics of shock incarceration as a scare method point out that offenders placed in shock incarceration are likely to lose their jobs or have family relationships severed in result (Clear, Reisig, & Cole, 2016).

An additional form of intermediate sanction administered by correctional institutions is boot camp (Stohr, Walsh, & Hemmens, 2009). The use of *boot camp* is similar in purpose to the use of shock incarceration. Boot camps are designed to teach youngsters discipline and respect through a paramilitary curriculum that includes physical labor, intense workouts, and a regimented schedule. Evidence that boot camps are ineffective to reduce recidivism comes from a number of empirical studies concluding that more resources must be placed in reentry programs to directly target the needs of offenders returning to their communities (Parent, 2003).

LEARNING EXERCISES

- Create a chart to separate intermediate sanctions based on the administering agency; then, rate those that appear to be more effective in reducing recidivism.
- Identify the goals of corrections represented by each one of the intermediate sanctions listed in the chapter.

BIBLIOGRAPHY

Austin v. US, 847 A.2d 391 (D.C. Cir. 2004).

Bazemore, G. (1998). Restorative justice and earned redemption: Communities, victims, and offender reintegration. *American Behavioral Scientist, 41*(6), 768–813.

Clear, T. R., Reisig, M. D., & Cole, G. F. (2016). *American corrections*. Boston, MA: Cengage Learning.

Cohen, T. H. (2012). *Pretrial release and misconduct in federal district courts, 2008–2010.* US Department of Justice, Office of Justice Programs, Bureau of Justice Statistics. NCJ 239243.

Cullen, F. T., Jonson, C. L., & Nagin, D. S. (2011). Prisons do not reduce recidivism: The high cost of ignoring science. *The Prison Journal, 91*(3_suppl), 48S–65S.

Morris, N., & Tonry, M. (1991). *Between prison and probation: Intermediate punishments in a rational sentencing system*. New York, NY: Oxford University Press.

O'Leary, V., & Newman, D. J. (1970). Conflict resolution in criminal justice. *Journal of Research in Crime and Delinquency, 7*(2), 99–119.

Parent, D. G. (2003). *Correctional boot camps: Lessons from a decade of research*. Washington, DC: US Department of Justice, Office of Justice Programs, National Institute of Justice.

Pepin, D., Hoss, A., & Penn, M. S. (2015). Menu of State batterer intervention program laws. Office for State, Tribal, Local and Territorial Support, Center for Control Disease & Prevention.

Schafer, S. (1970). *Compensation and restitution to victims of crime* (No. 120). Patterson Smith Publishing Corporation.

Schenwar, M. (2014). *Locked Down, Locked Out: Why Prison Doesn't Work and how We Can Do Better*. San Francisco, CA: Berrett-Koehler Publishers.

Stohr, M., Walsh, A., & Hemmens, C. (2009). *Corrections: A text/reader* (Vol. 3). Thousand Oaks, CA: Sage.

Ulrich, T. E. (2002). Pretrial diversion in the federal court system. *Federal Probation Journal,*, *66*, 30.

Welch, M. (2013). *Corrections: A critical approach*. New York, NY: Routledge: New York, NY.

Asset Forfeiture

Key and torn paper with text asset forfeiture on wooden background

THE RIGHTS OF AMERICANS AND THE GOVERNMENT'S USE OF CIVIL FORFEITURE

The imposition of fines as a form of punishment is not a new concept. Scholars have traced the origins of these practices to ancient civilizations (Gurule, 1995; Rulli, 2016). Despite the widespread use of civil forfeiture in the past, limitations were clearly specified in the law, as to make sure that fines were proportionate to the offense and would not deprive the offender of the means to live (Rulli, 2016).

As earlier discussed, America's founding fathers were influenced by European penal reformers of the 18th century. Among them was Cesare Beccaria who believed that punishment to be effective must be proportionate to the crime. This principle is embedded in the Eighth Amendment. Although the exact meaning of "excessive fines" was not specified at the time the Eighth Amendment was written, there is a general understanding that the Excessive Fines Clause of the Eighth Amendment directly limits the power of the U.S. government to demand payments from an offender as a form of punishment (Rulli, 2016).

In 1993, the U.S. Supreme Court ruled in *Austin v. United States* that civil forfeiture constitutes a form of punishment that is subject to the limitations imposed by the Excessive Fines Clause of the Eighth Amendment. Five years later, in *United States v. Bajakajan*, the U.S. Supreme Court held that "a punitive forfeiture violates the Excessive Fines Clause if it is grossly disproportional to the gravity of a defendant's offense" (Rulli, 2016: 1117). Despite the Supreme Court's decisions, many civil forfeiture cases occurred during the era known as the War on Drugs in the United States. In most cases, defendants were low-income minorities unable to have the means to protect their property from the abuses of the criminal justice system (Rulli, 2016).

Civil asset forfeiture actions are enforced when probable cause exists that a property was involved in an illegal activity. Because the practice does not require that the owner is charged with a crime, the property is often confiscated and never reported, avoiding any formal scrutiny under the Eighth Amendment Excessive Fines Clause (Rulli, 2016). These practices became legally justified under the 1978 Amendment to the Comprehensive Drug Abuse Prevention and Control Act of 1970 that allowed law enforcement to forfeit money or property. In addition, in 1984, Congress further amended the Act to extend the use of civil asset forfeiture to family homes and allow law enforcement agencies to cash the proceeds from the sales. Without any doubt these practice became high priority among many law enforcement agencies and many abuses were denounced at the expenses of a number of innocent individuals (Rulli, 2016).

Rulli (2016) proposes that courts follow a constitutional test when assessing the relevance of cases and proceed with a logical inquiry. The constitutional test would involve an *assessment of the instrumentality of the property*, *culpability of the property owner*, *proportionality*, *harm to the community*, and the *consequences of the asset forfeiture*. More specifically, per Rulli (2006):

- The test of instrumentality of the property would require that the nexus between the property and the crime be made clear; in addition, it would require a clear explanation of how the property in question truly facilitated the crime.

- The test of culpability of the property owner would allow investigating the owners' involvement in the crime before depriving them of their property.

- The test of proportionality would require that the relationship between the offense and the property value be verified.

- Furthermore, an assessment of whether the offense caused harm to the community would be necessary.

- Finally, the consequences of the property's seizure on the individual's livelihood and that of his/her family would need to be ascertained.

On January 16, 2005, following the exposure of many unjustified cases of civil forfeiture during the War on Drugs, the Obama administration issued an order to prohibit civil asset forfeiture by federal agencies except for public safety reasons (United States Department of

Justice, 2015). The Trump administration has recently reversed the Obama's administration decision. Attorney General Jeff Sessions provided a justification for lifting the limitations imposed by the previous administration citing the concerns over the opioid epidemics and suggesting that the threat of civil asset forfeiture would allow law enforcement agencies to leverage the collaboration of informants in the local communities (United States Department of Justice, 2017).

BIBLIOGRAPHY

Austin v. United States (1993). 509 U.S. 602, 113 S. Ct. 2801, 125 L. Ed. 2d 488.

Gurule, J. (1995). Introduction: The ancient roots of modern forfeiture Law. *Journal of Legislation*, *21*, 155.

Rulli, L. S. (2016). Seizing Family Homes from the Innocent: Can the Eighth Amendment Protect Minorities and the Poor from Excessive Punishment in Civil Forfeiture. *The University of Pennsylvania Journal of Constitutional Law*, *19*, 1111.

United States Department of Justice (2015). *Attorney General Prohibits Federal Agency Adoptions of Assets Seized by State and Local Law Enforcement Agencies Except Where Needed to Protect Public Safety*. Justice News: Department of Public Affairs.

United States Department of Justice (2017). *Attorney General Jeff Sessions Updates United States Attorneys and DOJ Component Heads on the Department's Task Force on Crime Reduction and Public Safety*. Justice News: Department of Public Affairs.

United States v. Bajakajian (1998). 524 U.S. 321, 118 S. Ct. 2028, 141 L. Ed. 2d 314.

Section IV

Jails and Detention Facilities

CIRCA 2002 - Entrance to Cook County Department of Corrections, Chicago, Illinois

CHAPTER 9

Jails

Man holding jail bars

LEARNING OBJECTIVES

- Describe the evolution of the jail in America
- Discuss the various problems associated with modern jails in the United States
- Identify the connection between jail design and philosophies of social control

INTRODUCTION

One might perceive that jails have always existed. The need to hold people in a secure space while awaiting trial characterized the history of both ancient and modern social systems (Kerle, 1998). The jail can certainly be considered as a precursor of the prison. While its scope has always been different from that of the prison, throughout history jails have provided an example of incarceration on which the prison has been designed. However, jails have a more diverse mission than prisons.

Jails usually serve local communities, such as municipalities and counties, and are operated by law enforcement agencies (most often by the county Sheriff's department). According to Cornelius (2012), "jails are defined as locally funded and operated correctional facilities that are centrally located in a community" (p. 390). While the idea of the local jails might evoke images of small facilities, some county jails house very large numbers of individuals in overcrowded facilities. An example of very large and overcrowded county jails often mentioned in research studies is Cook county jail located in Chicago, Illinois (Abram & Teplin, 1991; Lamb & Weinberger, 1998).

Just like prisons, jails have experienced an increase in intake numbers throughout the years of the War on Drugs (Stohr, Walsh, & Hemmens, 2009). In addition, after the massive shutdown of mental health hospitals around the nation, jails have become warehouses for individuals suffering from severe mental illnesses in need of care (Baillargeon, Binswanger, Penn, Williams, & Murray, 2009).

A BRIEF HISTORY OF JAILS

The American jail is modeled after the English "gaol"—a facility meant to house "vagrants, drunkards, the poor, trespassers, children, debtors, murderers, and dissenters with the church" (Cornelius, 2012: 392). *Gaols* were directly funded through the payment of fees imposed on those detained, but corrupted officials often pocketed the fees while failing to provide necessities to the inmates. Squallor, degradation, and often death characterized the *gaols* of the English tradition.

In America, the first jail complex was established in the Jamestown Colony of Virginia. Many new jails were built during the 17th century throughout the colonies. The fee-based system continued and corruption was rampant. Inmates in colonial jails were forced to work under slavery conditions (Cornelius, 2012).

European prison reformers like John Howard and Benjamin Rush became instrumental for the revolutionary ideas that founded the Philadelphia's Walnut Street Jail in 1773. Inmates were subjected to a regimented schedule that involved labor, reflection, and confinement (Cornelius, 2012).

While the Walnut Street Jail was a successful model, much of the efforts were applied toward the expansion of penitentiaries for convicted offenders in the main urban areas of the new world (Philadelphia, Pittsburgh, and New York are of-cited examples). Jails, on the other hand, remained neglected (Cornelius, 2012).

The expansion of jails continued all throughout the 1800s in America. While jails were often considered "useful" by criminal justice experts, a federal investigation conducted in 1923 found that most jails were kept in horrible conditions. Standards have been developed for jail operation and inmate management and care by national associations (the American Correctional Association and the National Commission on Correctional Health Care). Jails do not have to adopt the standards, but in most cases, the adoption and compliance with standards helps jail administrators prevent lawsuits (Cornelius, 2012).

JAIL ARCHITECTURE

An introduction to the different jail architecture styles is relevant to understand how social control can be expressed via the design of correctional facilities. Three types of architectural styles are present in U.S. colonial and modern jails: linear, podular, and cell-block designs (Stohr, Walsh, & Hemmens, 2009). In many modern jails, the three styles coexist within the same facility. The architecture of the jail (or jail wing) most often matches the philosophy of supervision implemented within the institution (Mays & Winfree, 2014).

- *Linear designs* were considered as the first generation of the jail, with long straight corridor and cells lined up on one side; these jails were meant to maintain order within the jail with minimal supervision.

- Similarly, *podular designs* would have a round shape with a control tower in the middle of the facility overlooking all the cells. This design was modeled after the Panopticon, a sort of utopia prison where inmates would be under constant surveillance as nobody could hide from the complete view granted by the presence of a central control tower.

- The most modern jail design is the *third generation jail* with direct supervision; within this design, officers monitor offenders in a common area with no physical barriers. This form of supervision is considered more humane and allow for congregation with other inmates.

While all three designs are often present within the same facility, different areas of the jail house different types of offenders. The linear, podular, and cell block designs, or other combinations of these, are used differently depending on the philosophy of social control of the jail (Clear, Reisig, & Cole, 2018). For instance, a podular design is often used for individuals suffering from severe mental health problems that require constant surveillance to prevent suicide. Instead, a cell block type of area allows for inmates who are not a threat to others to move around the facility (Stohr, Walsh, & Hemmens, 2009).

1. Linear design

© AdrianoK/Shutterstock.com

Prison cells in California

2. Podular design – like panopticon

Interior detail of the old jail " Presidio Modelo ", Nueva Gerona, Cuba 2010.

3. Direct supervision

Prison Cells at Alcatraz Island Cell Block A.

MODERN JAILS

While jails have historically being used to detain offenders awaiting trial, the function of the jail has evolved in modern history. Today, jails house very different groups of individuals (Clear, Reisig, & Cole, 2018; Mays & Winfree, 2014; Stohr, Walsh, & Hemmens, 2009):

1. Individuals awaiting their first court hearing, trial, or sentencing.
2. Violators of probation, parole, or military deserters awaiting transportation to military facilities.

3. Individuals suffering from severe mental illnesses pending court action or awaiting transfer to specialized facilities.

4. Individuals awaiting transfer to immigration detention centers (under ICE) or other facilities under the supervision of the Department of Homeland Security.

5. Individuals awaiting extradition.

6. Convicted state and federal offenders under specific programs (see, for instance, the California realignment program) aimed to ease the problems associated with prison overcrowding.

JAIL POPULATION

In a recent report, the Prison Policy Initiative provides a count of local correctional facilities showing that currently the United States has 3,163 local jails, 80 Indian country jails and numerous other detention centers (Wagner & Sawyer, 2018). A snapshot of the correctional population indicates that jails in the United States hold 1 every 3 incarcerated individuals. A total of 731,000 jail inmates were counted in 2018; among them, 615,000 were held in jails for local authorities, while 116,000 were held for other authorities (Immigration Customs Enforcement, Marshalls, or State Prisons). Of the 615,000 held in for local authorities, 464,000 were non-convicted. Of the 150,000 held post-conviction, 46,000 were incarcerated for public order offenses, 35,000 for drug offenses, 37,000 for property offenses, and 32,000 for violent offense.

Wagner & Sawyer (2018) estimated that more than 10 million people are admitted to local jails every year in the United States, a number large enough to "[…] fill a line of prison buses bumper-to-bumper from New York City to San Francisco" (p. 7). While these numbers seem high, since 2008, the jail population continues to decline. For instance, the jail incarceration rate per 100,000 residents declined from 259 inmates in 2008 to 229 inmates in 2016 (Zeng, 2018). However, estimates from the Bureau of Justice Statistics highlight relevant differences by gender and race. By the end of 2016, women had a jail incarceration rate of 62 inmates per 100,000 residents while men had a rate of 377. Blacks had the highest incarceration rate with 599 inmates per 100,000 residents. Native Americans also had high rates of jail incarceration with 359 inmates per 100,000. These rates compare to 171 inmates per 100,000 residents among Whites and 185 inmates per 100,000 for Hispanics/Latinos (Zeng, 2018).

JAIL CONDITIONS AND INMATE MORTALITY

On average, jail inmates are expected to stay in the facility for about 25 days. The turnover is very high in local jails, with smaller jails showing the shorter length of stay and higher turnover than larger jails (Zeng, 2018). However, one of the major problems jail administrators face is overcrowding. Many jails around the United States operate above their 100% capacity; that is, they house more inmates than the original number of beds would allow (which is commensurate to the size of the facility). While 17% of jails in 2016 operated above the 100% rated capacity, the overall number of beds assigned during 2016 went down from 95% in 2007 to 80% in 2016 (Zeng, 2018).

Among the many issues associated with overcrowding, the problem of sexual assault is the most concerning. Estimates from 2012 found that at least 3% of all adult jail inmates reported sexual assault while in jail. Rates of sexual assault were three times as high among juveniles (Bureau of Justice Statistics, 2017). In 2003, the Prison Rape Elimination Act (PREA) provided guidelines for the prevention of sexual assault in correctional facilities. In addition, PREA also required that rigorous studies be developed to investigate sexual assault among incarcerated individuals. In corrections as much as in society, sexual assault is under-reported. The high numbers represented in jails and prison surveys warrant attention.

The number of people dying in custody is still very high in the United States (Noonan & Ginder, 2015). While the jail population has been decreasing, rates of death while in custody have risen in recent years. For instance, Bureau of Justice Statistics' estimates show that, although the jail population declined by 4% between 2012 and 2013, rates of mortality increased by 3%, from 128 deaths per 100,000 inmates in 2012 to 135 deaths per 100,000 inmates in 2013. The leading causes of death among jail inmates were suicide and heart disease. According to Noonan and Ginder (2015), in 2013 over one third of all jail inmates who died while in custody died by suicide. During that year, the jail suicide rate was 40 suicides per 100,000 inmates.

LEARNING EXERCISE

For discussion:

A review of the existing studies highlights that the conditions of the local jails have not improved much in modern era, what are some of the possible remedies to change this scenario? As you prepare to discuss this, it might be important to be reminded that county budgets tend to be very tight.

BIBLIOGRAPHY

Abram, K. M., & Teplin, L. A. (1991). Co-occurring disorders among mentally ill jail detainees: Implications for public policy. *American Psychologist*, *46*(10), 1036.

Baillargeon, J., Binswanger, I. A., Penn, J. V., Williams, B. A., & Murray, O. J. (2009). Psychiatric disorders and repeat incarcerations: the revolving prison door. *American Journal of Psychiatry*, *166*(1), 103–109.

Bureau of Justice Statistics (2017). Prison Elimination Act of 2003. PREA data collection activities, 2017. U.S. Department of Justice. Office of Justice Programs. Bureau of Justice Statistics. NCJ 250752.

Clear, T. R., Reisig, M. D., & Cole, G. F. (2018). *American corrections*. Boston, MA: Cengage Learning.

Cornelius, G. F. (2012). Jails: Pretrial detention, and short-term confinement. In J. Petersilia, & K. R. Reitz (Eds.), *The Oxford handbook of sentencing and corrections* (pp. 389–415). New York, NY: Oxford University Press.

Kerle, K. E. (1998). *American jails: Looking to the future*. Burlington MA: Butterworth-Heinemann.

Lamb, H. R., & Weinberger, L. E. (1998). Persons with severe mental illness in jails and prisons: a review. *Psychiatric services*, *49*(4), 483–492.

Mays, G. L., & Winfree Jr, L. T. (2014). *Essentials of corrections.* Wiley Blackwell, Malden, MA.

Noonan, M., & Ginder, S. (2013). *Mortality in local jails and state prisons, 2000–2011, statistical tables.* Washington, DC: US Department of Justice, Office of Justice Programs, Bureau of Justice Statistics.

Stohr, M., Walsh, A., & Hemmens, C. (2009). *Corrections: A text/reader* (Vol. 3). Sage, Thousand Oaks, CA.

Wagner, P., & Rabuy, B. (2016). Mass incarceration: The whole pie 2016. *Prison Policy Initiative, 14.*

Zeng, Z. (2018). Jail Inmates in 2016. U.S. Department of Justice, Office of Justice Programs, Bureau of Justice Statistics. NCJ 251210.

CHAPTER 10

Detention Centers

Barbed wire detention center at countryside and background sepia color style cowboy

INTRODUCTION

The term "detention center" is most often used to refer to any facility administered (directly or indirectly) by an agency of the federal government to imprison individuals who are suspected to have violated U.S. laws. Detention centers vary greatly depending on the government agency exercising control. Currently, the two most debated types of detention centers in current media are military detention centers and immigration detention centers. The former under the supervision of the military (Department of Defense). The latter under the supervision of immigration authorities or Immigration Custom Enforcement (ICE). Public opinion and support for the control exercised by both the military and immigration agencies is often polarized. Conservative voters and politicians tend to be more likely to support the detention of illegal immigrants for reasons that are labelled as "public safety concerns." Progressive (or liberal) voters and politicians tend to be more likely to express concerns about the conditions of detention and the rights of detainees held in custody.

MILITARY DETENTION CENTERS

Following the terrorist attack of September 11, 2001, the U.S. government created a number of "black sites," detention centers located in undisclosed areas of the country and abroad. These centers were used to conduct thorough investigations to identify those responsible for the attack that killed over 3,000 and injured 6,000 more (Coda & Lawton, 2016; Del Rosso, 2014). Within these centers, the U.S. military and the CIA subjected detained suspects to a rigid interrogation protocol known as Enhanced Interrogation Tactics (EIT). The main controversy over the use of black sites began in 2004 when photos of abuses against detainees inside the Abu Ghraib facility (Iraq) were leaked to the press and became known to the public, causing a major public outrage both at home and abroad. Some argue that the main issue was not that abuse was used to interrogate detainees but that this became a public matter. Perhaps the intent to hide rather than eliminate torture became clear when the military banned the use of photography during war operations (Van Dijck, 2008).

An Independent Committee appointed by the U.S. Senate Select Committee on Intelligence conducted an investigation on the CIA operations during the years following 9–11. A

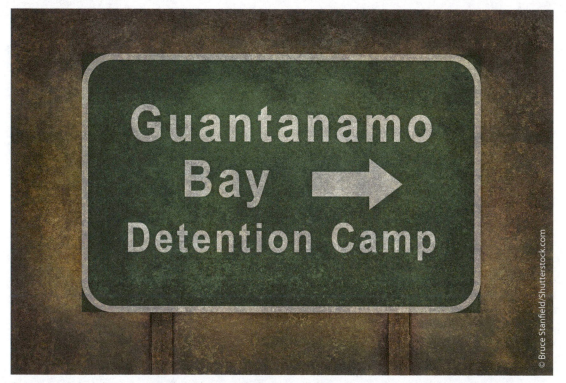

Guantanamo Bay detention camp road sign with directional arrow, illustration with distressed ominous background

final report made available in 2014 summarized the main findings of the Committee, concluding that the CIA used special interrogation tactics that led to either false confessions or no confessions at all. In addition, the same interrogation techniques contributed to the death of several detainees while in custody (United States Senate, 2014). In 2006, President George W. Bush signed the Military Commission Act (MCA) after it was approved by Congress. In the MCA, the Bush administration defined detainees as *"unlawful enemy combatants"* with no right to counsel and/or appeal. Two cases brought before the U.S. Supreme Court, *Halmadi v. Rumsfield* and *Boumediene v. Bush*, clarified that non-American detainees under the supervision of the U.S. government maintain the writ of *habeas corpus* which permits to question the legality of their detention. The writ of *habeas corpus* is the main protection detainees have against systematic and unjustified abuses of government authorities while detained or incarcerated.

Despite the success of legal cases in the decisions of the U.S. Supreme Court, concerns over the detention of suspected terrorists and the treatment of detainees in military detention centers managed by U.S. government agencies continue to be debated both within the country and abroad (Coda & Lawton, 2016; Del Rosso, 2014).

IMMIGRATION DETENTION CENTERS

The term "immigration detention center" most often refers to centers supervised by federal immigration authorities, such as the U.S. Department of Homeland Security and Immigration and Customs Enforcement (ICE). The role of immigration detention centers

has become more relevant in the last two decades. In 1996, the Illegal Immigration Reform and Immigrant Responsibility Act reclassified numerous law violations previously listed as misdemeanors as felonies (e.g., shoplifting and minor drug offenses). Consequently, many immigrants apprehended for violations of the law in recent years have been detained in immigration detention centers awaiting deportation. In addition, because the statute gave authorities the power to apply the law retroactively, many immigrants with prior criminal records became easy target for detention and deportation procedures (Welch, 2011).

Detention centers are often forgotten by the public. Facilities are away from the public eye and stories about immigrants detained and deported are often neglected in media reports. As Welsh points out "[l]ocked behind bars in criminal jails, limited in their English language ability, and fearing possible deportation, immigration detainees are both physically and emotionally isolated" (2011: 382). Despite these policies, immigrants in the United States, even those considered "illegal aliens," have rights. In a recent position paper, the American Civil Liberties Union (ACLU) explains that although the government has the right to decide who can enter the country, once here, all immigrants (even undocumented immigrants) have the right to freedom of speech and religion, the right to privacy, and other fundamental rights granted by the U.S. Constitution (ACLU, 2018). In 1903, in *Yamataya v. Fisher*, U.S. Supreme Court ruled that immigration authorities cannot deport someone without due process. People facing deportation have the right to:

1. have their case reviewed by a judge;
2. be represented by a lawyer (at their own expenses);
3. receive notice of the charges and details about the hearing (time and place);
4. have an opportunity to examine the evidence and the government's witnesses;
5. adequate interpretation for non-English speaking immigrants;
6. clear proof that the grounds for deportation are valid.

One of the major limitations undocumented immigrants face in deportation cases is access to counsel. In the United States, deportation is generally ruled by civil law, therefore, most individuals involved in deportation cases do not have right to counsel (as the Sixth only applies to criminal cases). According to Eagly & Shafer (2015), only about a third of all immigrants in the United States are able to secure representation. Among those in detention, only 11% are able to secure counsel. Recently, some scholars have argued that, while undocumented immigrants have rights, evidence exists that many of them are deported without due process (Sidhu & Boodoo, 2017). Many deportation cases are resolved very quickly through the "expedited removal process." Noncitizens under expedited removal process can only avoid deportation if they request asylum or express fear to return to their home country because of the threat of violence. Under current law, the Department of Homeland Security is required to refer the immigrant in custody to an asylum officer appointed by the U.S. Citizenship and Immigration Services. If the office finds the fear legitimate, the asylum seeker can discuss the claim before a judge. According to the Center for Migration Studies, the number of fear claims have risen in recent years (CMSNY, 2013).

LEARNING EXERCISES

The two links to the Frontline PBS website feature recent documentaries on the use of detention facilities by the U.S. government.

- Kirk, M (2015). Secrets, Politics, and Torture: https://www.pbs.org/wgbh/frontline/film/secrets-politics-and-torture/
- Young, Rick (2011). Lost in Detention (2011): https://www.pbs.org/wgbh/frontline/film/lost-in-detention/

After watching the documentaries, prepare a list of questions (4–6 question) for group discussion.

BIBLIOGRAPHY

American Civil Liberties Union (2018). The rights of immigrants – Position paper. Available at www.aclu.org

Boumediene v. Bush. (2008) 553 U.S. 723, 128 S. Ct. 2229, 171 L. Ed. 2d 41.

Center for Migration Studies. (2013). Congressional hearings on asylum seekers facing US expedited removal process. Available at www.cmsny.org

Coda, E. & Lawton, B. (2016). Re-visioning terrorism: The rack focus response. In Coda, E., & Lawton, B. (Eds.), *Re-visioning terrorism: A humanistic perspective*. West Lafayette, IN: Purdue University Press.

Del Rosso, J. (2014). The toxicity of torture: The cultural structure of US political discourse of waterboarding. *Social Forces*, *93*(1), 383–404.

Eagly, I. V., & Shafer, S. (2015). A national study of access to counsel in immigration court. *University of Pennsylvania Law Review*, *164*, 1.

Hamdan v. Rumsfeld. (2006). 126 S. Ct. 2749, 165 L. Ed. 2d 723.

Sidhu, S. S., & Boodoo, R. (2017). US case law and legal precedent affirming the due process rights of immigrants fleeing persecution. *The Journal of the American Academy of Psychiatry and the Law*, *45*(3), 365–373.

The Japanese Immigrant Case, (1903). 189 U.S. 86, 23 S. Ct. 611, 47 L. Ed. 721.

United States Senate (2014). *Report of the Senate Select Committee on Intelligence Committee Study of the Central Intelligence Agency's Detention and Interrogation Program, Together with Foreword by Chairman Feinstein and Additional and Minority Views*. DC. Available at https://fas.org/irp/congress/2014_rpt/ssci-rdi.pdf [last accessed on 03-14-2018].

Van Dijck, J. (2008). Digital photography: communication, identity, memory. *Visual Communication*, *7*(1), 57–76.

Welch, M. (2011). *Corrections: A critical approach*. New York, NY: Routledge.

A Case Study of Immigration Detention

Stories of illegal immigration are not uncommon in the United States. Among the stories that reached the media, that of "Henry" seems particularly troublesome. Henry is a teenager detained in the Hudson County Correctional Facility in New Jersey because of his affiliation with the notorious gang MS-13.

Henry is originally from El Salvador where he lived with his grandparents for most of his life. Henry's parents left home to come to the United States when he was very young. By age 11, Henry had already joined the gang. In his community, joining the gang is not a choice. Kids seek protection and the gang is the only option. The gang is there to protect the families, provide food, money, or other things they need. When kids join the gang, they have to go through an initiation process that includes witnessing the killing of another person. At age 15, Henry realized that the life of the gang was too much for him. Henry decided to cross the borders and seek asylum in the United States. He managed to enter the country legally and felt relieved at the idea of starting a new life.

In 2014, Henry started school and he finally felt his life was changing for the better. Unfortunately, a member of the MS-13 in Long Island recognized him and the gang wanted him back. He was punished for leaving and abandoning the gang. Henry had to subordinate to the gang's rules once again. As a member of MS-13, Henry had to report any interaction with members of rival gangs. One day, a girl name Kayla Cuevas confronted him in school. She stared at him and threw the signs for the *Bloods* (another notorious gang active in the United States). He had to report her to MS-13 members. Days later, the news came out that Kayla was dead; as the News reported, "she fell victim of gang violence."

More than anything, Henry wanted the violence to stop. He decided to talk about his issues with one of his high school teachers and mentors. This particular teacher was compassionate and wanted to help Henry get out of the gang. To help him find protection from MS-13, she decided to call the police. Henry collaborated with the police; he provided information about the people the gang was planning to kill. He became an informant. Following state statute, the police officers contacted ICE and Henry was arrested. All the gang members whose names he disclosed were also arrested and detained in the same facility. While in detention, Henry received many death threats. For people like Henry, running away from the gang might mean death. While the story of Henry reached the American media, there are reasons to believe that there many youths like Henry struggling to survive.

*This story was adapted from the article:

Dreier, H. (2018). The Betrayal of Triste. *Propubblica* and *New York Magazine*, April, 2018. Interview transcription from https://features.propublica.org

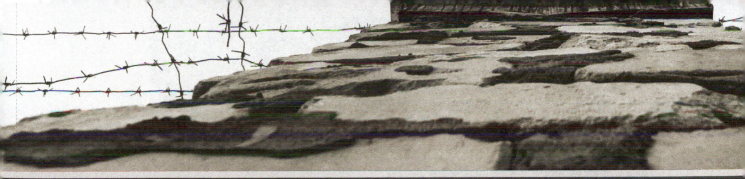

Section V

Prisons

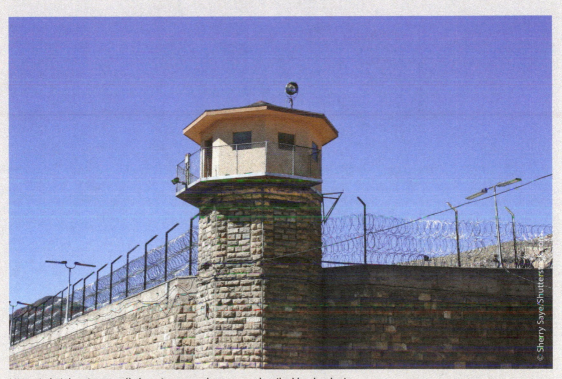

Historic brick prison wall showing guard tower and coiled barbed wire

CHAPTER 11

History of Prisons

Stockholm, Sweden - July 10, 2012: Prison bars and hands. Urban sculpture in Stockholm, Sweden

LEARNING OBJECTIVES

- Articulating the history of the first prisons in the new world
- Describing how new philosophies of punishment led to the creation of the prison
- Discussing the changes that occurred in the management of inmates throughout the United States
- Explaining how historical events outside the prison led to a culture of mass-incarceration

INTRODUCTION

Many changes occurred in North America during the fifty years following the 1776 Declaration of Independence. Building a system that would guarantee "justice" to all citizens became a priority of the free world. As Thomas Jefferson stated, "the most sacred of the duties of a government [is] to do equal and impartial justice to all its citizens" (as quoted in Oliver & Hilgenberg, 2010: 81).

While many of the social and political engineers of the United States advocated for principles of equality and justice as fundamental values of a new society, many of these values remained part of the national discourse but were never fully implemented. As Oliver and Hilgenberg (2010) discussed, several of those who signed the Declaration of Independence believed that including women and non-whites was not necessary.

THE COLONIAL ERA (1776–1828)

During the American Colonial Era, a significant transformation of the system of punishment and corrections reflected the changes captured in the Declaration of Independence. Freed from the control of the British government, the former colonies could design their own system of punishment. Important reforms began in Pennsylvania in the late 1770s through the commitment of Quakers like Ben Franklin, Benjamin Rush, and William Bradford. In 1786, the new Penal Code redefined the crimes punished through capital sentences and allowed for the conversation of several felonies punishable with hard labor and public service (Oliver & Hilgenberg, 2010). Meanwhile, Rush also advocated for the abolition of the death penalty, a very progressive idea that has never been accepted unanimously in the United States. With fewer offenders sentenced to death for capital crimes, the need for the creation of a permanent carceral system became apparent.

Scientists trace back the beginning of the prison era to the conversion of the Newgate's copper mine (Connecticut) in 1773 to detain offenders. Citing a document of the American Correctional Association titled "American Prison: From the Beginning…A Pictorial History," Welch (2011) provides a detailed description of this first unique facility. As Welch put it, "[t]he prison consisted of three parallel excavated caverns, about 800 feet long and approximately 25 feet below the surface and one pool of fresh water. The administration buildings were built over the mineshafts" (2011: 55). Corporal punishment was commonly used to discipline inmates. Perhaps the reader is not surprised to learn that, as a consequence of the conditions under which prisoners were housed in the facility, violence and riots became a daily problem (Welch, 2011). Prison historians and sociologists agree that the Newgate, CT prison marks a turning point in the treatment of offenders in the United States. A point in history that connects Colonial America to the U.S. criminal justice system and the idea that incarceration can become a productive practice when prisoners are put to work. Labor was indeed recognized as both as profitable way to support the prison and an effective method of rehabilitation for offenders by instilling work ethic (Durham, 1989; Welch, 2011). The Newgate, CT facility was later replaced with the Wethersfield facility in 1820, as the costs associated with the operation of the facility became unsustainable (Welch, 2011). The Wethersfield facility remained in operation until 1963 (Hartford Courant, 2008).

Pennsylvania also contemplated many changes in its system of punishment. The deplorable conditions of the Walnut Street Jail in Philadelphia at the end of the Revolutionary War (1973) led to a comprehensive reform designed by the Quakers (Gray, 1973; Welch, 2011). In 1786, the Pennsylvania legislature authorized, for the first time in the history of the United States, the allocation of funds for the construction of a prison. The Walnut Street Jail in Philadelphia became the first jail to function based on the penal reform and to be used for long-term detention. In 1790, the jail became a state penitentiary but it continued to serve for both purposes of pre-trial detention and long-term confinement (Oliver & Hilgenberg, 2010). Although the Quakers' humanitarian principles are most often mentioned in reference to the restructuring of the Walnut Street Jail, some prison historians argue that there was also a serious attempt to use the reformed prison as way to centralize and control the state penal reform, a political maneuvering seen as strategic for the era (Takagi, 1975).

Continuous changes were implemented in the Walnut Street Jail throughout the 1790s. The jail became the model of penal reform not only in the United States but also in Europe where a widespread number of governments recognized the inefficiencies of penal systems based on the use of corporal punishment and capital punishment. Among the most relevant changes implemented in the Walnut Street Jail were:

- Banning alcohol
- Using labor to rehabilitate offenders
- Separating juveniles from adults
- Including a system of classification based on "danger"
- Establishing a prison school to educate offenders

Unfortunately, overcrowding quickly became a major issue and the conditions of incarceration deteriorated within the jail, leading to prison protests and revolts that forced the administrators of the jail to keep inmates inside their cells, in idle under strict surveillance (Oliver & Hilgenberg, 2010).

An analysis of the problems affecting prisons and jails in contemporary societies might suggest that penal systems that use confinement as a way to punish law-breakers still struggle with the same issues that affected the very first prison in the world.

A plea for the construction of new penitentiaries came from the Philadelphia Society for Alleviating the Miseries of Public Prisons which formed in 1787 specifically to advocate for the human rights of inmates confined in the Walnut Street Jail under harsh conditions (Michel, n.d.). However, it was not until the late 1820s that two new penitentiaries opened: Western Pennsylvania in Pittsburgh and Eastern Penitentiary in Cherry Hill near Philadelphia (Oliver & Hilgenberg, 2010).

The New York system faced problems similar to those of the Philadelphia system and the Newgate jail built in 1797 soon became overcrowded. The Auburn penitentiary opened in 1817. Inmates deemed as "most dangerous" were kept in solitary confinement. No labor was allowed for those in solitary confinement and inmates were required to stand the whole day in their cells. Under such duress, many inmates' mental health began to deteriorate causing many management challenges due to violent behaviors and a spike in suicides. As consequence of these problems, Auburn adopted a philosophy of "congregation" for the daytime and solitary confinement for the night time. While inmates worked in congregation, they were not allowed to talk to one another. Hand signals were required to communicate with the guards. Religion was mandatory and it was used as a main method for the redemption of offenders. Physical punishment was used to correct their behavior any time a violation of prison rules occurred. The system was praised for keeping inmates under control. However, in 1925 the New York legislature requested that inmates would be required to work more in order to make more profits, necessary to supporting the high costs of the facility (Oliver & Hilgenberg, 2010). A very important innovation in the Auburn penitentiary was the "tier system," a structure where cells were separated on different levels, allowing for the segregation of inmates by offense category (Lewis, 1922; Welch, 2011).

In 1827, the New York legislature authorized the expansion of the state penal system through the construction of a new penitentiary on Mount Pleasant: Sing Sing (Cheli, 2003). The penitentiary was built entirely by Auburn's inmates, under the supervision of Elam Lynds who was later appointed as the warden of the facility. Lynds used a militaristic style to discipline offenders and corporal punishment was the main instrument to control inmates. Flogging was deemed as an effective method of keeping the prison population under control. The penitentiary was soon recognized as a utopia as the results were very different from those their proponents advocated for (Welch, 2011).

The two systems of Philadelphia and New York were similar in many ways. However, criminal justice experts point out that:

> "The Pennsylvania system was built with the Quaker religion in mind. Part of this religion was the belief that people could change, that they could be reformed and therefore become productive citizens. The New York system, on the other hand, was not constructed with any specific religious principles in mind, and those running the prison were less inclined to believe anyone could be reformed." (Oliver & Hilgenberg, 128)

THE JACKSONIAN ERA (1829–1855)

Under Andrew Jackson's presidency, poverty, mental health problems, and criminality were all seen as social maladies that needed reforms and interventions (Welch, 2011). Crime was seen as a threat to social order and effective ways to curb its impact were sought throughout the Jackson's era (Rothman, 1971). Both the family and the community became the focal points of social control policies implemented under President Jackson (Rothman, 1971; Welch, 2011). With Jackson, both the Pennsylvania and the New York prison systems became very popular around the country and in Europe; however, problems associated with overcrowding, corruption, and brutality became apparent very quickly. New penitentiaries opened in the rest of the United States during the 19th century (Oliver & Hilgenberg, 2010).

A typical issue experienced in all the cities and states that pioneered the establishment of the penitentiary was that the prison management inefficiencies that followed the most notable penal reforms became very difficult to fix. An unstable economy, political transitions, and wars all constituted priorities over the conditions of the prisons in America. A significant effort toward the inefficiencies of the prison came to fruition with the "Report on the Prisons and Reformatories of the United States and Canada" published by Enoch Cobb Wines (secretary of the New York Prison Association) and Theodore Dwight (first President of the

Columbia School of Law). The report analyzed data from a survey of numerous institutions of corrections and concluded that the American penal system was in need of a reform centered on principles of justices, fairness, and human rights (Oliver & Hilgenberg, 2010).

While the report became a very important source, the authors became extremely influential after organizing a series of conferences to allow for brainstorming sessions on the reform of the prison system. Most states participated in these conferences. Many influential speakers were invited to the sessions, including reformers Zebulon R. Brockway and Sir Walter Crofton. The National Congress on Penitentiary and Reformatory Discipline held in Cincinnati on October 11–12, 1870 provided 37 detailed principles to guide the much needed reform of the penal system. Following the conferences, the legislature approved the funds to build the Elmira Reformatory and Zebulon R. Brockway was appointed as its superintendent. The reform included the use of indeterminate sentences and the rehabilitation of offenders.

While applauded for his innovative ideas, Brockway was destined to become a controversial figure as the use of corporal punishment through industrial labor education at the Elmira's reformatory was known to be quite harsh (Oliver & Hilgenberg, 2010). In "The American Reformatory Prison System," published in 1910 in the *American Journal of Sociology,* Brockway discussed the ideology that guided the reform. Brockway used a reward system that applied a military disciplinary style founded on the idea of reformation and rehabilitation of the offender (Brockway, 1910).

The controversy over the abuses against inmates led to Brockway's resignation in 1900, after New York's Governor Theodore Roosevelt appointed three new managers to investigate the issue that had become of national interest (Oliver & Hilgenberg, 2010).

The events surrounding the Elmira's scandal perfectly fit in the idea that prison was there to save society. Prisons and reformatories were part of the "utopia" that affected social engineers and prison reformers alike during the 1800s (Pollock, Hogan, Lambert, Ross, & Sundt, 2012). Crime was seen as the symptom of social degeneration and the prison was considered the main instrument to save society from the continuously rising crime rates (Rothman, 1971; also cited in Pollock, Hogan, Lambert, Ross, & Sundt, 2012).

THE POST CIVIL WAR ERA

As it often happens with major wars, during the Civil War there was no money set aside for social programs. Once again, the conditions of prisons and the need of offenders were not a priority. During the war, many prisons both in the North and South of the country became war camps. Shortage of supplies caused many prisoners to die.

After the civil war, the country had to be rebuilt and there were not enough resources to focus on the restructuring of the penitentiaries (Oliver & Hilgenberg, 2010). Poverty and disorders among civilians in the South led to a huge increase in the rates of both property and violent crimes.

The penitentiary and the reformatory experiments were mainly a phenomenon of the North and the Midwest. In the South, the constructions of correctional facilities developed more slowly. But the South had to deal with the intolerance and lack of trust that white people had against the former slaves. The social divide between whites and the freed slaves led to a fast rise in rates of incarceration for blacks, especially young black men; a trend yet to be corrected in the U.S. criminal justice system (Welch, 2011). Penal farms were used as correctional institutions with the convict leasing program adopted as a system where inmates were forced to work to serve private companies. Prisoners worked under very harsh conditions with chains around their ankles, were fed poorly, and abused (Oliver & Hilgenberg, 2010). The emphasis on prison labor ended during the Depression era because of the spike in unemployment rates throughout the nation. Workers organizations and labor unions demanded the end of the convict labor. Two new pieces of legislation passed at the Federal level to prohibit the shipment of prison manufactured goods in the private sector: the Hawes-Cooper Act, 1929 and the Ashurst-Sumners Act, 1935 (Welch, 2011). The program was converted into a public labor program in which inmates worked toward the improvement of public goods. Under this newly designed labor system, inmates built and maintained public roads (Oliver & Hilgenberg, 2010).

While some see these changes as the result of the shift in economic opportunities and the need to protect the employment of law-abiding citizens (Ignatieff, 1978; Melossi & Pavarini, 2018; Welch, 2011); others consider the end of the convict lease as an innovation toward the protection of inmates and the prevention of inmate exploitation (Oliver & Hilgenberg, 2010).

THE 20TH CENTURY

The first two decades of the 1900s are known to criminal justice experts as the "progressive era" because of all the changes that occurred within the U.S. system of punishment and corrections, changes that focused on the protection of inmates and a newly designed ideology on rehabilitation.

Within the penitentiary, the focus shifted from the crime to the individual and an analysis of needs would be used to identify the most appropriate rehabilitation program for each offender. More moneys were invested to hire specialized counselors, case managers, and psychiatrists to support the new goal of rehabilitation. As expected, however, the program became unsustainable and the focus on rehabilitation quickly faded (Oliver & Hilgenberg, 2010). Once again, penitentiaries became warehouses where inmates had no opportunity for rehabilitation.

THE FEDERAL SYSTEM

In 1930, the Federal Government created the Federal prison system: the U.S. Bureau of Prisons, under the supervision of the U.S. Justice Department. One of the first federal penitentiaries built in the United States was the notorious "Alcatraz," a maximum security prison built on a rocky island off the San Francisco Bay in California. Due to the enormous costs associated with the transportation of both people and goods from the mainland to the island and back, the penitentiary was closed in 1963 (Oliver & Hilgenberg, 2010). Once designed for the incarceration of high-risk offenders, Alcatraz is now a museum.

© Click Images/Shutterstock.com

THE PRISONER RIGHTS' MOVEMENT

Throughout the 1950s and 1960s, prisoner rights' movements proliferated around the country, advocating for better treatment, better conditions, and justice. As Oliver and Hilgenberg (2010) point out, the 1950s were characterized by the presence of several riots. The numerous social changes that occurred throughout the 1960s in the United States led to a new ideology of prison reform: the era of reintegration, primarily focused on offender reentry. This phase focused on inmates maintaining their constitutional rights as the U.S. Supreme Court confirmed in the historical 1964 decision in *Cooper v. Pate.* Thomas Cooper, an inmate confined in the Illinois State Prison located in Joliet, near Chicago, was denied his rights to read religious books because he was Muslim (*Cooper v. Pate*, 1964). The lawsuit against the Warden of the facility, Frank Pate, became an important law to set a precedent in inmate litigation. The Supreme court ruled that "just because a person is imprisoned does not mean that he or she will lose their constitutional rights" (Oliver & Hilgenberg, 2010: 300).

The decision in *Cooper v. Pate* provided an opportunity for re-examining the Civil Rights Act of 1871 which granted the President of the United States the power to suspend the writ of habeas corpus when necessary to combat the KKK (Gressman, 1952; Wright, 1995). While the 13th Amendment of the U.S. Constitution abolished slavery and involuntary servitude, one would could still be considered a slave of the state following his conviction for a crime (Gilmore, 2000). In addition, *Cooper v. Pate* overturned the Supreme Court decision in *Ruffin v. Commonwealth*, according to which "[a] convicted felon has, as a consequence

Old Joliet Prison, Joliet, IL

of his crime, not only forfeited his liberty, but all of his personal rights except those which the law in its humanity accords him. He is for the time being a slave of the state" (*Ruffin v. Commonwealth*, 1871).

The 1964 decision in *Cooper v. Pate* became the starting point for a new era of inmate lawsuits. As Oliver & Hilgenberg (2010) point out, throughout the three decades that followed *Cooper v. Pate*, an estimate of 25,000 lawsuits a year were filed by inmates throughout the United States.

THE 1980s AND THE CLOSURE OF MENTAL HEALTH INSTITUTIONS

An important change that influenced the penal system for many years, and it still plagues contemporary jails and prisons in the United States, was the closure of mental health institutions in the 1980s. In most cases, mental health hospital in the United States operated with small budgets; consequently, patients were kept in deplorable conditions. The idea behind the shutdown of all the inadequate facilities was to promote family support and reintegrate individuals with mental health problems and intellectual disabilities back into societies, surrounded by caring family members. Meanwhile, a major shift in prison's reform occurred. The era of reintegration quickly faded as crime rates sore between the 1960s and the 1980s.

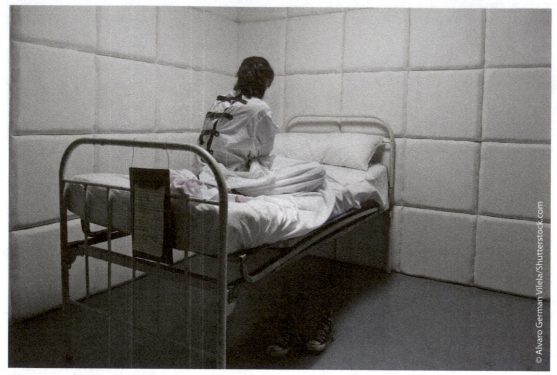

Crazy with a straitjacket in a Psychiatric

The era of retribution began, reshaping the U.S. correctional system for several decades. This shift led to a new era of prison expansion that critics labelled as the era of "mass-incarceration" (Alexander, 2011). The prison population grew by 500% during the 40 years between 1970 and 2010, reaching 2.3 million inmates. As previously discussed, the War on Drugs' legislation implemented during the 1980s caused an unprecedented expansion of the prison system that disproportionately affected low income communities, especially communities with predominantly non-white residents (Mauer & King, 2007; see also West, Sabol, & Greenman, 2010).

A common denominator among all the prison reforms, (including the closing of mental health institutions and the establishment of separate reformatories for women and children), is the good intention behind the ideas led by social engineers throughout the history of the United States. Inescapably, however, these reforms transformed institutions of corrections into chaotic, overcrowded, corrupt, and abusive agencies of the criminal justice system leading to a massive expansion of the population under state and federal supervision (Pollock, Hogan, Lambert, Ross, & Sundt, 2012).

The creation of the Juvenile Justice System became one of the most important innovations of the 19th century. The first group to advocate for the reformation of abandoned children was the Society for the Prevention of Pauperism of New York, established in 1816 and renamed Society for the Reformation of Juvenile Delinquents in 1820 (Oliver & Hilgenberg, 2010).

THE DEVELOPMENT OF A SEPARATE SYSTEM FOR JUVENILES

While this manuscript does not focus on juvenile offenders, a brief overview of the juvenile reformatory and the establishment of a separate juvenile justice system is relevant to the discussion on punishment and corrections. The principles behind the creation of a specialized justice system for youth developed in line with those of the adult system of punishment and corrections.

Like the adult penitentiary system, the juvenile reformatory movement was based upon principles of humanitarian aid as advocated by benevolent groups led by Quakers. A review of history documents reveals that compassion for children was needed during the first decades of the new world. As per the English Law tradition, in Colonial America children older than age 7 years were treated as harshly as adults within the criminal justice system. Punishment included detention, corporal punishment, and even execution (Schwartz, Travis, & Clear, 1997). Industrialization and the expansion of urban areas caused the weakening of "mechanism of social control" (Bernard & Kurlychek, 2010). In other words, as parents worked shifts in factories to provide for their families, children were often left behind in the neighborhood with other children, neglected by adults. The economic expansion of the 19th century and the growth of manufacturing sector influenced the rapid growth in the population of major cities like New York, Philadelphia, and Chicago. For instance, the urban population of Philadelphia grew by 365% between 1850 and 1860 (Bernard & Kurlychek, 2010).

The first House of Refuge opened in 1825 in New York but other cities in the United States followed the example and Houses of Refuge were established in Boston and Philadelphia as well (Oliver & Hilgenberg, 2010). In 1893, with *Reg v. Gyngell,* 4 R 450, the court established the legal process to transfer the custody of a child to the court (Matthews & Maund, 1895). The court would be invested of the *parens patriae* and act in *loco parentis* (Latin for "on behalf of parents"). The child would then become ward of the court, a process that would give the judge the authority to commit the child to the House of Refuge (Ferdinand, 1991).

As Seymour highlighted:

"That was not a jurisdiction to determine rights as between a parent and a stranger, or as between a parent and a child. It was a paternal jurisdiction, a judicially administrative jurisdiction, in virtue of which the Chancery court was put to act on behalf of the Crown, as being the guardian of all infants, on the place of a parent, as if it were the parent of the child, thus superseding the natural guardianship of the parent."(1994: 159)

The idea that the court would supersede the authority of the parents appears rooted in principles of English Common Law. This was not a common practice in Ancient Rome where family law was formalized. The Romans would leave the absolute power to discipline children to the father who had the *patria potestas* as children were seen as property (Buti, 2003). The House of Refuge became a common institution across the United States during the first half of the 1800s. However, Houses of Refuge were not perfect place. Similarly to the conditions of jails and prison that housed adult offenders, Houses of Refuge for juveniles became quickly overcrowded and abuse was rampant. While youth reformatories were created to protect youth from becoming prey for adult offenders, the adults in charge of the Houses of Refuse often abused children in custody. Black children were often neglected and as a consequence of increased rates of poverty among blacks, in 1849 Philadelphia opened the House of Refuge for Colored Juvenile Delinquents. Only a few years later, in 1956 the Massachusetts State Industrial School for Girls opened to support girls in need of a "mothering environment" (Oliver & Hilgenberg, 2010: 160). The trend to round up kids for lack of parental supervision, the orphans, and the immigrants became concerning. A case that was brought to the Illinois Supreme Court in 1870, ruled that committing juveniles who did not offend to youth reformatories was unconstitutional (Malekian & Nordlöf, 2012).

It was not until 1899 that the first juvenile court was established in Chicago. Jane Addams, who founded the Hull House in the city, is today recognized as one of the most influential advocates for the wellbeing of underprivileged children (Moyer, 2008). The court was deemed rehabilitative rather than punitive and would support delinquent children younger than 16 years of age. By 1925, the juvenile system became established across the United States (Oliver & Hilgenberg, 2010). Throughout the 1950s and 1960s, new efforts to improve the juvenile justice system emphasized the focus on rehabilitation rather than punishment. However, the most important legal changes became knowns as *In re Gault* (1967) and *In re Winship* (1970). In the 1967 decision *In re Gault,* the U.S. Supreme Court ruled that juveniles in court must be afforded the same treatment as adults, they must be granted counsel, and informed of the charges. In the 1970 decision *In re Winship*, the U.S. Supreme Court held that juveniles – like adults – must be found guilty beyond reasonable doubt and that the preponderance of evidence is not sufficient in delinquency cases.

The era between 1985 and 1995 could be labeled as the "dark era" for juvenile justice as the ramifications of the War on Drugs and the tough on crime policies contributed to the spike in rates of arrest and detention among urban youth, especially minority youth in large metropolitan areas. The widespread panic over the responsibility of juvenile delinquents in violent cases contributed to the increase in cases of youth waived to adult courts (Oliver & Hilgeberg, 2010).

A more recent effort funded by the Anne E. Kasey Foundation and established in many jurisdiction around the country focuses on reducing the number of children detained pre-adjudication. This effort is known as Juvenile Detention Alternatives Initiative or JDAI and it has contributed to the reduction in youth detention rates and positively impacted rates of re-offending among youth (Mendel, 2009; Sherman, 2005).

THE HISTORY OF PRISONS FOR WOMEN

In addition to establishing a separate Juvenile Justice System, a women's prison reform began to develop during the 19th century. Women's incarceration was not common until the 1840s. Women were sometimes held in local jails and the existing penitentiary would at times house women in remote areas of the building, sometimes in the attic. Incidents of rape and forced prostitutions within penitentiaries became known to the public. Women support groups formed in Philadelphia, New York, and Baltimore to help women confined in the penitentiaries. Differently from the traditional penitentiaries built for men, women's prisons were built according to a cottage-style where women would circulate and organize themselves in labor activities with fewer constraints (Oliver & Hilgenberg, 2010).

Prison historians report that the first prison for women was built in Indiana in 1873. The prison was first named the "Indiana Reformatory for Women and Girls" but it later became known as the Indiana Women's Prison. Michelle Jones and Lori Record, who conducted an historical investigation of archived documents in the library of the same facility during their long-term incarceration, argue that the first prisons for women were the Catholic institutions originated in Ireland and known as "Magdalene Laundries" which served as private institutions of corrections for women accused of sex-related offenses (Jones & Record, 2017).

While prostitution was rampant during the years after the Civil War, official records of the prison did not include women sex offenders. Jones and Record wondered where would the sex offenders be incarcerated if not in the only women's prison in their state. Traditionally, the Laundries existed for the isolation of women and girls deemed unruly, those who became pregnant out of wedlock or those who were themselves born out of wedlock. Prostitutes and lesbians would often find themselves in these institutions that were meant for washing their sins and rehabilitate them. Girls and women deemed unfit for mainstream society were most often placed in these institutions by their families, their churches, or by the courts (Jones & Record, 2017).

Using data from the U.S. Census, Jones and Record provide the reader with a list of 39 Magdalene Laundries institutions opened in the United States between 1843 and 1899, all maintained by the Sisters of the Good Shepherd, a Catholic order of nuns. Using Rothman's definition of prison which consider prisons as places of separation, obedience, and labor, Jones and Record (2017), analyzed the characteristics of the Laundries to categories these institutions established for the isolation and redemption of women and girls rejected by mainstream society for their inability to conform to gender norms or expected gender roles. As Jones and Record specify (2017: 174–5).

While the Magdalene Laundries are not included in the history of prisons, they presented many of the characteristics of the modern prison.

1. Like offenders incarcerated in the contemporary prison, women confined in the Laundries were sentenced by criminal courts.

2. Women in the Laundries were deprived of their identities, their property, and even their own names.

3. Women were confined in the Laundries against their will. Similar to offenders in the contemporary prison system, some of them spent years and some even spent their entire life in the Laundries.

4. The Laundries were disconnected from the outside world and restrictions were applied to both the circulation of mail and visitations.

5. The architectural structure of the Laundries was very similar to that of the modern prison, including the cells, the barred windows and even the barbed wire to prevent escapes.

6. Various forms of punishment were used in the Laundries for violations of the rules imposed by the administration.

7. Solitary confinement in small size cells was not uncommon and just like in modern prisons it was used as a form of punishment.

8. Women had to observe a very structured routine.

9. Some of the most experienced women within the Laundries were in charge of the order. These women were known as "solidarity sisters" and were expected to supervise other women in the facility, similar to what trustees do within modern correctional facilities.

10. Confinement in the Laundries was a source of stigma for the women and reentry into society was as difficult as it is for incarcerated offenders today.

The argument Jones and Record (2017) put forward has merit for several reasons. First, if the Magdalene Laundries operated as prisons, we must include them in the history of all prisons. Failing to include the Laundries in the history of corrections might mean to accept a gross under representation of women and girls incarcerated throughout the history of the United States. Moreover, by excluding the Laundries from the history of American corrections, we might be avoiding looking into the conditions of confinement to which many women and girls were subjected and the abuses they endured.

LEARNING EXERCISES

- Create a chart that summarizes the American prison system's timeline with the main changes occurred since its inception.

- Compare and contrast the two penal systems in the North: the Pennsylvania and the New York system.

- Discuss how major shifts in the U.S. economy, due to wars or other significant changes, led to changes in the penal system.

BIBLIOGRAPHY

Alexander, M. (2011). The New Jim Crow. *Ohio St. J. Crim. L.*, *9*, 7.

Bernard, T. J., & Kurlychek, M. C. (2010). *The cycle of juvenile justice.* New York, NY: Oxford University Press.

Brockway, Z. R. (1910). The American reformatory prison system. *American Journal of Sociology*, *15*(4), 454–477.

Buti, A. (2003). The Early History of the Law of Guardianship of Children: From Rome to the Tenures Abolition Act 1660. UW Sydney L. Rev., 7, 91.

Cheli, G. (2003). In Senate, Report: From the Commissioners for building a new prison at Sing Sing. Archadia Publishing, Charleston, SC.

Cooper v. Pate, 378 U.S. 546, 84 S. Ct. 1733, 12 L. Ed. 2d 1030 (1964).

Durham, A. M. (1989). Origins of interest in the privatization of punishment: The nineteenth and twentieth century American experience. *Criminology*, *27*(1), 107–139.

Ferdinand, T. N. (1991). History overtakes the juvenile justice system. *Crime & Delinquency, 37*(2), 204–224.

Gilmore, K. (2000). Slavery and prison—understanding the connections. *Social Justice, 27*(3 (81), 195–205.

Gray, F. C. (1847). *Prison discipline in America* (Vol. 3). Boston : C. C. Little and J. Brown, 1847. Available through the University of California Library.

Gressman, E. (1952). The unhappy history of civil rights legislation. *Michigan Law Review, 50*(8), 1323–1358.

Hartford Courant (2008). A prison where 73 inmates were executed. News Report, Available at http:// articles.courant.com/2008-02-13/news/0802120522_1_state-prison-new-prison-million-prison [last visited on May 21, 2018].

Ignatieff, M. (1978). *A just measure of pain: the penitentiary in the industrial revolution, 1750–1850.* New York: Pantheon Books.

Jones, M., & Record, L. (2017). Magdalene Laundries: The first prisons for women in the United States. *Journal of the Indiana Academy of the Social Sciences, 17*(1), 12.

Lewis, O. F. (1922). *The development of American prisons and prison customs, 1776–1845: With special reference to early institutions in the state of New York.* Prison Association of New York.

Malekian, F., & Nordlöf, K. (Eds.). (2012). *The sovereignty of children in law.* Tyne, UK: Cambridge Scholars Publishing.

Matthews, J. B. & Maund, A. A. (1895). *The law relating to children and young persons.* Sweet & Maxwell Ltd., Law Publishers, London, UK.

Mauer, M., & King, R. S. (2007). *Uneven justice: State rates of incarceration by race and ethnicity* (pp. 1–23). Washington, DC: Sentencing Project.

Melossi, D., & Pavarini, M. (2018). *The prison and the factory: Origins of the penitentiary system.* Springer.

Mendel, R. A. (2009). Two decades of JDAI: From demonstration project to national standard.

Michel, L. (n.d.). Pennsylvania Prison Society. In *The Encyclopedia of Greater Philadelphia.* Available at: http://philadelphiaencyclopedia.org/archive/pennsylvania-prison-society/ [last visited May 17, 2018].

Imogene L. Moyer MA, PhD (2008) Jane Addams, *Women & Criminal Justice*, 14:2–3, 1–14

Oliver, W. M., & Hilgenberg, J. F. (2010). *A history of crime and criminal justice in America.* Durham, NC: Carolina Academic Press.

Pollock, J. M., Hogan, N. L., Lambert, E. G., Ross, J. I., & Sundt, J. L. (2012). A Utopian Prison: Contradiction in Terms? *Journal of Contemporary Criminal Justice, 28*(1), 60–76.

Rothman, D. J. (1971). *The discovery of the asylum: Social order and disorder in the new republic.* Boston, MA: Little, Brown & Co. Publishers.

Ruffin v. Commonwealth, No. 2007-CA-000827-MR (Ky. Ct. App. Nov. 16, 2007).

Schwartz, M. D., Travis, L. F., & Clear, T. R. (1997). *Corrections, an issues approach.* OH: Anderson Publishing Company.

Sherman, F. T. (2005). Detention Reform and Girls: Challenges and Solutions: JDAI Pathways to Detention Reform# 13.

Seymour, J. (1994). Parens patrice and wardship powers: Their nature and origins. *Oxford Journal of Legal Studies*, *14*(2), 159–188.

Takagi, P. (1975). The walnut street jail: A penal reform to centralize the powers of the state. *Federal Probation Journal*, *39*, 18.

Walker, S. (1980). Popular justice: A history of American criminal justice. *Michigan Law Review*, *79*, 921.

Welch, M. (2011). *Corrections: A critical approach*. New York, NY: Routledge, New York, NY.

West, H. C., Sabol, W. J., & Greenman, S. J. (2010). Prisoners in 2009 (NCJ 231675). Washington, DC: Bureau of Justice Statistics, US Department of Justice.

Wright, P. (1995). Slaves of the state. *Journal of Prisoners on Prisons*, *6*(2), 17–20.

CHAPTER 12

Inmates and Life in Prison

Silhouette of man walking along a barbed wire high fence

LEARNING OBJECTIVES

- Describe the current prison population
- Provide an overview of theories focusing on inmates' life in prison
- Summarize research findings on prison adaptation and misconduct
- Discuss the challenges of housing inmates with special health needs

INTRODUCTION: OVERVIEW OF U.S. PRISON POPULATION

Americans have become accustomed to the idea that the United States incarcerates offenders at higher rates than those of other Western nations. Estimates from 2018 show that the U.S. adult prison system is comprised of 1,719 state facilities and 102 federal facilities (Wagner & Sawyer, 2018). Collectively, these correctional institutions hold an estimated population of 1.5 million with 1,316,000 inmates housed in state facilities (BJS, 2018; Wagner & Sawyer, 2018). Almost all the inmates in state and federal facilities are held for incarceration sentences longer than one year (BJS, 2018).

Among them, 718,000 (or 54.6%) are convicted of violent crimes, 237,000 (18.0%) are incarcerated for property offenses while 200,000 (15.2%) are there for drug offenses. In total, 152,000 inmates (or 11.5%) are incarcerated in state facilities because of public order offenses. Finally, 9,000 of all the state offenders are incarcerated for offenses classified as "other" offenses (Wagner & Sawyer, 2018). The current picture shows that more than half of all state offenders are incarcerated because of a violent offense. Considering that incarceration rates have fallen in the past 10 to 12 years, it is possible that the current picture reflects a conscious effort to reduce the prison population by prioritizing the confinement of violent offenders while redirecting non-violent offenders to other forms of supervision. For instance, recent reports suggest that alternative forms of corrections focus on offenders suffering from substance abuse and mental health problems through specialized courts and community-based corrections (Entry, 2013).

A breakdown of all violent offenders in state prisons shows that 180,000 inmates (out of 718,000, or 25.1% of all violent offenders) are incarcerated for murder. In addition, 24.2% of all violent offenders (164,000) were sentenced for rape or sexual assault. Robbery is the third largest category of offenses among all violent offenders in state correctional facilities, with 174,000 offenders convicted of robbery, representing 19.2% of all violent offenders in state facilities. Inmates incarcerated on assault charges were 19.2% of all violent offenders (138,000 inmates). Finally, 44,000 inmates (6.1% of all violent offenders) are incarcerated for crimes classified as "other" (Wagner & Sawyer, 2018).

At the end of 2016, rates of incarceration were 450 prisoners per 100,000 U.S. residents of all ages and 582 prisoners per 100,000 residents 18 years or older. These estimates also lead to a conclusion that during the same year, roughly 1% of all adult males in the United States were serving a sentence in prison (BJS, 2018). An analysis of the prison population by race shows that among male prisoners, 39% were white, 41.3% were black, 16.6 Hispanic, 1.4% were American Indian or Alaskan native, .6% were Asian, and 1.1% were of other races (Carson, 2018). Next, the focus is on the characteristics of women incarcerated in the United States. While men represent more than 90% of the whole prison population, the incarceration of women is equally concerning.

WOMEN IN PRISON

Since the beginning of the War on Drugs' legislation, women and girls' incarceration rates have grown faster than men's incarceration rates. Estimates from the Bureau of Justice Statistics show that during the 1980 to 2010 period, rates of incarceration for women grew by over 600%

Social issues, abuse and violence on women. Depressed girl, sad African American young woman crying at home. Abused and scared wife

(The Sentencing Project, 1986). More recently, Carson (2015) reported that at the end of 2014 there were 106,200 women incarcerated in U.S. State and Federal correctional facilities, representing 7.3% of all individuals in adult state and federal correctional facilities (Carson & Anderson, 2016).

Differently from men, women are more likely to be incarcerated for non-violent offenses, such as, drug offenses, property offenses, and public order offenses. As shown consistently in criminological research, women are less likely than men to be violent and to be convicted to a prison sentence for violent behaviors. At the end of 2013, 37.1% of all women incarcerated were classified as violent offenders as compared to 54.4% of all men in state department of corrections (Carson, 2015).

Minority women, especially black women, tend to be overrepresented among inmates. Carson (2015) point out that, in 2014, black women were incarcerated at rates twice as high as those of white women; in addition, Hispanic women were 1.2 more likely to be incarcerated than white women.

Incarcerated individuals, in general, tend to be young. Recent estimates indicate that 28% of women in state and federal correctional facilities are below the age of 30, compared to 27.8% of men (Carson, 2015).

Within the state prison population, women are more likely than men to be parents. Estimates indicate that 61.7% of women incarcerated in U.S. state prisons are parents of minor children compared to 51.2% of men in state facilities. The situation, however, appears different in federal facilities where 63.4% of men and 55.9% of women are parents of minor children (Glaze & Maruschak, 2008). The incarceration of women, however, appears to be more problematic than that of men when it comes to parenthood. Data from the Bureau of Justice Statistics show that women incarcerated are most often solely responsible for their children prior to their imprisonment. Data from 2008 show that 41.7% of women in state prisons lived with their children as solo parents, while only 17.2% of men in state prisons reported similar circumstances (Glaze & Maruschak, 2008).

Women offenders tend to be less recidivistic than men offenders. According to Langan and Levin (2002), while more than one third of all men incarcerated are re-admitted to a correctional facility within 5 years from their release, only 12% of women inmates are re-admitted to prison within the same period of time (Langan & Levin, 2002). Women, however, are more likely than men to become re-incarcerated as a consequence of technical violations of their parole agreement. Feminist scholars denounce current policies as inadequate to support the needs of women on parole or probation who struggle to support their children and comply with the rigid structure of rules of community supervision (Holtfreter & Morash, 2003; Kruttschnitt, 2010).

Although a history of poverty and lack of emotional support are common among both female and male offenders, women are more likely than men in prison to suffer from the consequences of abuse. Recent studies show that more than 40% of women incarcerated were abused prior to their last incarceration compared to 7% of men (Solinas-Saunders & Stacer, 2012). Understanding abuse is important because rates of mental health problems among women offenders are often the direct consequence of the abuse endured during childhood, adolescence, or young adulthood. Research estimates indicate that about half of all women incarcerated suffer from some form of mental illness compare to about a quarter of all men (Solinas-Saunders & Stacer, 2012).

Unfortunately, a period of incarceration does not boost a woman's ability to stay off trouble. Unemployment is a major problem for many individuals who end up in the criminal justice system and prison do not prepare offenders to deal with the challenges of low income communities. For women, the inability to provide for their children contributes to their involvement with the law (Giallombardo, 1966; Owen, 1998). Prison programs offered in women's facilities mostly focus on traditional "women's occupations, such as food preparation, catering, and cosmetology, failing to prepare women to go back to the outside world and become self-sufficient (Morash, Bynum, & Koons-Witt, 1998).

Research on incarcerated women has also provided knowledge about women's sexuality and their ability to form intimate relationships while in prison. Early studies on women's sexuality in prison were traditionally framed across racial lines, describing white women in prison as delicate and vulnerable individuals at the mercy of black female inmates acting as predators (Otis, 1913). In 1931, Selling pioneered a different approach to the study of women's relationships in prison focused on the complexity of family-like alliances within groups. Following Selling's model, studies on the prison "pseudo-family" proliferated throughout the United States (Giallombardo, 1966; Ward & Kassebaum, 1966). These studies prioritized an analysis of feminine and masculine roles in women's prisons and explored the social hierarchy established among women incarcerated. While research on women's relationships in prison reflect the need to explore even further the emotional needs of women incarcerated, much of the existing studies tend to separate issues of sexuality from the other personal issues women face while confined in institutions of corrections. This might be indicative of a widespread tendency to trivialize sex as a less deserving aspect of human life, especially women's life. While a growing body of research focuses on women's sexual exploitation in prison and experience with rape and abuse, research is needed to understand how relationships form in prison among women inmates and women's ability to support one another during confinement.

ADAPTATION TO PRISON AND INMATE MISCONDUCT

In the last 50 years, the overcrowding of correctional institutions has become a major concern among scientists and policy makers. Overcrowding brings many challenges in the management of prisons. Proving the necessary programs to fulfill the rehabilitation mission is certainly one of the main problems. In addition, overcrowding tends to limit a facility's ability to deal with disruptive inmates. Zero tolerance policies and the federalization of drug crimes have led to the incarceration of different types of individuals, from the drug addict to violent gang members, often housed within the same correctional facility (Gaes, Wallace, Gilman, Klein-Saffran, & Suppa, 2002). For correctional administrations, reducing the incidence of prison misconduct is a priority, as the mission of any institution can (ideally) be effectively reached only when internal order is maintained.

Four African American youths in a Southern chain gang. Southern jails made money leasing convicts for forced labor in the Jim Crow South. Circa. 1900

Sociologists and criminologists have focused on prison adaptation from several different angles. In other words, the literature on adaptation provides studies that focus on inmates' prosocial behaviors, such as participation in formative programs and other pro-social group activities (Lahm, 2008, 2009; Solinas-Saunders & Stacer, 2012). In addition, the literature on adaptation also focuses on the actual lack of adaptation, such as misconduct (Morris & Worrall, 2014; Steiner & Wooldredge, 2008, 2009).

In his early work, Clemmer (1940) provided us with important insights in the life of inmates and their tendency to conform to the institutional norms as defined by the prison population; a phenomenon of resocialization within institutions of corrections that Clemmer labeled as "prisonization." Adding to Clemmer's relevant exploratory narrative on prisoners' life, Sykes (1958) argued that inmates' prison experiences develop in function of the facility. Per Sykes' observations, inmates' responses to the prison deprivation vary little among individuals. In this view, the prison itself becomes the main determinants of an inmate's experience during incarceration. While Sykes focused on the individual (microanalysis of incarceration), Goffman (1961) provided us with another unique perspective that prioritize the role of the prison as a system of social control. Goffman (1961) described prisons as "total institutions." In his influential work on the dynamics that develop within rigid and unforgiving social systems, Goffman compares prisons to other bureaucracies like mental health institutions and the military. Within these social systems, the strict and regimented routine and the vertical communication of orders is meant to exercise an absolute form of control to maintain order. While many inmates participate in prison programs that often involve interactions with professionals from the outside (lawyers, counselors, medical staff, and tutors), prisons today still represent total institutions in that inmates are deprived of their ability to make decisions for themselves and are subjected to the continuous exercise of institutional supervision. The rigidity of Goffman's total institutions provides us with an example of bureaucracy that is meant to create a system of deprivation and hurt those sentenced to incarceration not just by limiting their physical mobility but especially their mind and soul (Foucault, 1977). The rigid bureaucratic structure of the prison can be examined in juxtaposition to the idea of freedom most often pursued by those most prone to break away from societal norms. If breaking free from socially imposed norms constitutes the norm itself, a familiar milieu or *habitus* (Bourdieu, 1990), the rigid structure of the prison becomes an insurmountable barrier to adaptation. The prison is an environment in which one's propensity to adopt illicit forms of contractual power flourish among those prone to succumb to the deliberate coercion of corruption which inevitably leads to a form of deviant adaptation.

These traditional hypotheses of prison adaptation, deprivation, and misconduct are today embodied in the two dominant theoretical perspectives on prison adaptation: the importation model and the functionalist model. The importation model posits that inmates' pre-prison experiences and their personal background tend to shape their prison experience (Irwin & Cressey, 1962). The functionalist model describes inmates' prison experiences as a function of institutional characteristics. Two separate versions of the functionalist model can be found in the contemporary prison literature: the deprivation model and the situational model. Per the deprivation model, inmates tend to have similar reactions to the deprivation of the prison environment. Differently, the situational model argues that specific characteristics of the institution tend to directly affect inmates, their behaviors, and their ability to conform with prison rules. Examples of prison situational characteristics explored in the literature are overcrowding, hours spent in segregation, number of people in a cell, and exposure to natural light. A more recent application of the functionalist models has allowed for the development of transfer theory which focuses on the effect that transferring inmates from one facility to another might have on their ability to adjust to institutional rules (Kigerl & Hamilton, 2016).

Another traditional theoretical approach to the study of prison misconduct is the management perspective. This approach focuses on the analysis of inmates' misconduct as a reaction to the management style and leadership model employed within the prison system. This approach has proven particularly useful for studies focusing on the macro level analysis of prison misconduct, allowing for a comparison across facilities based on their approach to leadership (Griffin & Hepburn, 2013).

Agnew's General Strain Theory (Agnew, 2001) has also been applied to explore prison misconduct. While this perspective was first developed through general exploratory studies of crime and deviance, applications of strain theory for the analysis of traumatic life transitions, such as incarceration, continue to contribute to the field of criminology by providing important insights on inmates' tendency to break rules in prison (Blevins, Listwan, Cullen, & Jonson, 2010).

While scholars define misconduct as a general tendency to break rules during incarceration, studies differ in the way they categorize the various forms of prison misconduct, such as verbal aggression, physical aggression, aggression against staff, aggression against other inmates, and minor violations versus serious violations. However, somewhat consistently, studies show that all types of misconduct in prison are associated with the same risk factors. Most commonly, sex (being male) and age (being young) tend to be strongly associated to prison misconduct. Studies also show that mental health problems tend to increase the risk for misconduct (Flanagan, 1983; Solinas-Saunders & Stacer, 2012). Spatial distance is also relevant in the analysis of prison misconduct. Inmates housed in facilities that are far from their own homes are also more likely to break prison rules (Cochran, 2012; Lindsey, Mears, Cochran, Bales, & Stults, 2015).

INMATE CLASSIFICATION

Within the U.S. correctional system, inmates are assigned to specific security levels (minimum, medium, or maximum) based on the nature of their offenses (Clear, Reisig, & Cole, 2016; Welch, 2011). Within each facility, inmates' propensity to re-offend, break rules or escape are measured to determine the appropriate intensity in supervision and surveillance (Bonta, 2002; Cunningham, & Sorensen, 2006). In addition, inmates' needs are assessed to identify key programs for rehabilitation (especially substance abuse programs, alcohol abuse programs, mental health programs, and educational programs) and suicide prevention (Gendreau, 1996; Gould, McGeorge, & Slade, 2017; Perry, Marandos, Coulton, & Johnson, 2010). The most common method for the assessment of inmates risk and needs is the use of actuarial measures, tools determined through predictive statistical estimations that make inference from large samples of offenders to identify behavioral patterns among the general prison populations (Gendreau, Goggin, & Law, 1997). Perhaps the main indicator of recidivism is the inmate's history of past crimes. However, the presence of other stressors might contribute to inmates' recidivism. For instance, history of unemployment and homelessness might also go hand in hand with mental health and substance abuse problems. One of the most difficult tasks in the management of offenders in correctional institutions is the co-existence of multiple problems and disorders (Draine, Salzer, Culhane, & Hadley, 2002). While predicting human behavior is very difficult as multiple factors contribute to the manifestation of an outcome, actuarial measures provide helpful tools to identify relevant programs, even though it is important to be aware of their limitations.

INMATE SPECIAL NEEDS IN PRISON

Drug abuse is a common problem among offenders. As Clear, Reisig, and Cole (2016) point out, while roughly 2% of the U.S. general population uses illegal substances, the majority of offenders who are arrested for a crime in major cities use drugs or were under the influence of

Elderly woman in prison

drugs at the time of the arrest. Crime and substance abuse often go hand in hand. While crime is often driven by the need to support one's habit, offenders who are substance abusers often become involved in serious crimes that involve the use of violence (Goldstein, 1985). Since the war on drugs legislation was implemented, institutions of corrections in the United States have been seriously involved in the management of drug offenders, both at the state and federal levels. However, as Clear, Reisig, and Cole (2016) point out, the results have been minimal. More recently, new initiatives tend to divert low-level offenders who are substance abusers to drug courts and in-patient treatment programs in the community (Ash, 2017). Drug and alcohol abuse are often the result of mental health problems among inmates. The most recent estimates (James & Glaze, 2006) from the Bureau of Justice Statistics point out that 56% of state inmates and 46% of federal inmates have either a current mental health problem or a history of mental health problems. Clear, Reisig, and Cole (2016) point out that there is also a general tendency to generalize abnormal behavior as the result of mental illnesses even when a disease of the brain is not observed. The surveillance and management of inmates suffering from mental health problems present serious challenges within institutions of corrections as providing appropriate training to all correctional staff is very costly (Lamb & Weinberger, 2005).

Prison inmates tend to present additional challenges as their health deteriorates during their incarceration. Aging in prison is of particular concern because older inmates tend to present more health care needs (Clear, Reisig, & Cole, 2016). Recent estimates, (Maruschak, Berzofsky, & Unangst, 2015) show that roughly one third of all inmates (about 30%) in prison have health chronic problems, such as hypertension. Two thirds of all inmates (66%) reported taking prescription medications while incarcerated. Women inmates were more likely than men inmates included in the sample to report suffering from at least one health chronic condition (25% of women compared to 20.7% of men). A comparison by race and ethnicity shows that white inmates were more likely than black inmates to suffer from chronic conditions (24.6% v. 16.7%). Hispanic offenders reported higher rates of chronic illnesses than all the other minority groups in prison (23.4%). The majoring of offenders in prison reported being either overweight or obese (62%). In addition, 21% of all prisoners reported ever having been diagnosed with either tuberculosis, hepatitis, or a sexually transmitted disease which included HIV and AIDS (Maruschak, Berzofskly, & Unangst, 2015).

While rates of HIV and AIDS among prison inmates are declining, with recent estimates showing that the prevalence of the virus and the development of the disease among prisoners is similar to that of U.S. residents, the management of HIV and AIDS patients in prison can be extra challenging (Clear, Reisig, & Cole, 2016). Estimates show that the costs associated with the care of AIDS patients in prison ranges between $50,000 and $300,000 per year. The typical AIDS patient in prison is low-level offenders with a history of intravenous drug use. While incarcerated AIDS patients present almost no risk to the communities, releasing destitute offenders with no housing, family, or community support to reduce the cost of incarceration does not seem to help our society at all (Clear, Reisig, & Cole, 2016).

One of the most challenging issues related to life in prison is the housing of transgender inmates. As the history of prisons teaches us, prisons were designed for men and some women. In prison, gender is conceived as a binary variable were male and female are seen as mutually exclusive (Jenness & Fenstermaker, 2014). The placement of inmates in gender appropriate correctional facilities is carried out on the basis of the inmate's sex, as assigned at birth. For inmates who identify as LGBT, prison dynamics might expose them to an increased risk of sexual abuse and victimization (Cowart, 2017). A survey conducted by the National Center for Transgender Equality in 2015 found that inmates who identified as transgender were six to 10 times more likely to experience both physical and sexual assault victimization during incarceration (James, Herman, Rankin, Keisling, Mottet, & Anafi, 2016).

Although prisons have very limited resources, state and federal governments alike have the obligation to protect inmates from the abuses that too often occur in institutions of corrections. Inmate-to-inmate assault and staff-to-inmate assault are very problematic issues in contemporary prisons. In 2003, Congress passed the Prison Rape Elimination Act (PREA) to provide specific standards and guidelines for the protection of inmates. PREA also provides intervention programs (medical and counseling services) for victims of sexual abuse (National PREA Resource Center, n.d.).

PRISON PROGRAMS

Prison programs have always been a highly debated topic. Those among us who support programs for inmates are concerned with the deleterious effect that idle inside institutions of corrections might have on offenders. Because prisons tend to house individuals with many specific needs, programs that address those needs have potential for reforming offenders by providing the necessary skills to become law-abiding citizens. On the other side of the argument are those concerned with the costs associated with offering prison programs and whether providing inmates with opportunities to learn new skills is fair to those in the outside who struggle to find meaningful employment and are unable to pay to pursue an education. Both sides of the argument have merit. Although it is true that resources are not unlimited and those who broke the law should not receive better opportunities than law abiding citizens, the purpose of prison programs is to help offenders find new pathways in life and prevent that further harm is done to society. In addition, the idea of "fairness" in the allocation of resources might require a much deeper analysis. On the other hand, many offenders have a history of marginalization that began early in life with negative experiences in schools and the community. The zero-tolerance approach implemented in many schools in the United States has led to what scholars have defined as the "school to prison pipeline." The presence of police in many schools has worsened the situation by allowing for an increase in rates of incarceration among youth. In addition, the trend is especially concerning for black youth who are 42% of all suspensions and represent 31% of all the school related arrests, although they are only 16% of those enrolled in school programs (Fabelo, Thompson, Plotkin, Carmichael, Marchbanks, & Booth, 2011). The children who get in trouble in school are often labeled as "antisocial" because are more likely to receive out of school suspensions, be arrested, or detained. These children, however, are more likely than their "pro-social" peers to suffer from learning disabilities, history of abuse and neglect, and also more likely to be poor and live in sub-standard living conditions (Loeber, Farrington, Stouthamer-Loeber, Caspi, White, Wei, & Beyers, 2003). When problems leading to antisocial behaviors are not addressed at young age, many children continue a path to offending that persists in adulthood (LeBlanc & Loeber, 1998). Living in an organized society might also mean that we take responsibility for those marginalized; hence, the meaning of fairness when it comes to support the offending population might not be as simple as many of us would like to think.

3D illustration of "DRUG REHABILITATION PROGRAM" title on medical documents. Medical concept

In the United States, correctional facilities vary in the number and type of programs they offer. The most commonly offered prison programs are substance abuse programs and educational programs. While states continue to experiment with different approaches to treatment in prison, measuring their efforts has proven difficult. One of the main issues in testing for effectiveness of prison programs is the inability of prison administrators (or reluctance) to assign inmates to programs by following randomized selection. The lack of random assignment in many studies introduces bias in research limiting researchers' ability to draw conclusions and make inference to the offending population (Belenko, Houser, & Welsh, 2012).

Drug treatment programs offered in state facilities vary by state but the Therapeutic Community (TC) is the most common model implemented across the United States. The typical TC model is based on a three-stage approach. The first stage is the orientation (usually during the first 3 months). The second stage is the main treatment (lasting for about 5–6 months). Finally, the third stage is the reentry preparation during which clients plan for the post-release maintenance. Some states also use follow-up treatments once offenders are released, which show higher levels of effectiveness (Belenko, Houser, & Welsh, 2012).

On average, offenders who suffer from substance abuse problems are more likely than offenders who do not use drugs to re-offend. This is perhaps explained by the fact that their criminality is strongly associated with their addiction. Inconsistencies in the implementation of TC programs within state facilities are often difficult to identify.

Additional programs showing promising results are those employing the medical approach. These programs use a pharmachological treatment, such as methadone for instance, that helps clients wean off the drug gradually over time. Medical treatment programs appear to be particularly effective among clients who are opioid users. Only a small fraction of all state prisons rely on the medical treatment approach (estimated to be less than 1%). The effectiveness of programs is measured either through data on re-offending (re-arrest and/or re-admission to prison) or through cost-benefit ratio analysis. In general, programs with the highest cost-benefit ratios are those targeting high-risk offenders (Belenko, Houser, & Welsh, 2012). This does not mean that low-risk offenders should not be treated, as low-risk offenders could become high-risk offenders or repeat offenders if left on their own and if their needs are not addressed. Because offenders/clients' substance abuse is often linked to past experiences with abuse, trauma, and marginalization, it would seem appropriate to focus on these issues through counseling sessions or peer support groups integrated in the treatment program. The association between mental health problems and substance abuse appears to be especially relevant among incarcerated women (Belenko, Houser, & Welsh, 2012).

Education programs are the most common programs inside U.S. federal and state correctional facilities, with over 90% of state facilities and all the federal facilities offering at least basic educational programs such as GED (Harlow, 2003). While the effectiveness of education programs has not been assessed through consistent research methods, the widespread acceptance of prison educational programs might reflect the belief that education is good in itself. In general, education helps improve one's self worth, comprehend and follow directions, complete basic tasks, and contribute to advance with more complex vocational skills. Educational programs were introduced to the prison for the first time by Zebulon R. Brockway in 1876 (Hanser, 2013; MacKenzie, 2012) and continued to be

Books in prison, concept of freedom of thought

implemented ever since. GED programs are the programs most available in correctional facilities across the nation. Considering that over 40% of state inmates are high-school dropouts (Harlow, 2003), offering GED courses seems appropriate. Some prisons partner with local universities to offer post graduate degrees. New Mexico, for instance, leads the nation with a state-wide initiative to offer long distance courses. The main challenge with online courses that inmates cannot surf the web. Creating a system that allows inmates to study using the learning management system of the granting institution without having access to other web sites can prove difficult and hard to manage as the facility needs tutors who can mediate the communication between the instructors and the incarcerated learners (Hanser, 2013; MacKenzie, 2012). The Pell grant program that was implemented to help indigent students complete their education was discontinued in 1994. Although the elimination of the Pell grant program initially discouraged participation in college programs in prison, current estimates show that the proportion of incarcerated people using post-secondary education programs is now similar to that of the Pell grant era, with approximately 5% of the correctional population currently attending college courses behind bars (Erisman & Contardo, 2005).

An initiative that began in Philadelphia in 1997 is the Inside-Out Prison Exchange program, now used in over 130 prisons and jails in North American and other parts of the world.

With Inside-Out (often abbreviated I-O), college instructors create courses that are taught in prison or jail facilities and are comprised of both inmates (inside students) and college students (outside students). The name Inside-Out stems from the idea that within the classroom, the two worlds of the prison and university become one entity where mutual exchanges among individuals occur. The I-O model follows the principles of experiential learning (Dewey, 1916; Freire, 1970) and provides opportunities for intellectual and social growth for instructors, inside students, and outside students alike (Davis & Roswell, 2013; Solinas-Saunders & Stacer, 2017).

Vocational programs are another common type of education-based programs. More than 50% of all state prisons and over 90% of federal prisons offer vocation programs (MacKenzie, 2012). Vocational programs are very different from one another. Some include basic education, such as literacy programs, life-skills programs, and labor skills (carpentry, plumbing, trade, among the most common). Because many vocational programs include follow-ups after release, through placement services, they tend to improve the chances to find employment which is linked to reduction in rates of recidivism (MacKenzie, 2012). While assessing what exactly works and why it works has been difficult because research studies on the use of vocational programs are rather sparse, empirical evidence exists that vocational programs that focus on changes within the individual tend to be more effective than vocational programs that focus on opportunities (MacKenzie, 2012).

Work programs are common in correctional facilities throughout the United States. Unlike educational and vocational programs, however, work programs do not directly target the mission of rehabilitation. Prison work programs are often used to curb the costs of prison maintenance (MacKenzie, 2012). In prison, inmates cook, clean, and often make uniforms and/or shoes. Federal prisons employ inmates for the production of plates and street signs (Hanser, 2013). While work in prison helps reduce idle and teach offenders how to stay on tasks, the literature on prison labor is filled with controversial issues, some already explored when discussing the history of the prison system in the United States.

LEARNING EXERCISES

Questions for group discussions:

1. What are the most challenging issues of life in prison for inmates?

2. The book does not focus on the role of correctional staff. Based on your understanding of inmates' needs, what would you say are the most challenging aspects of managing offenders in prison? Why? Explain your answers.

BIBLIOGRAPHY

Agnew, R. (2001). Building on the foundation of general strain theory: Specifying the types of strain most likely to lead to crime and delinquency. *Journal of Research in Crime and Delinquency*, *38*(4), 319–361.

Ash, M. E. (2017). *Living with harm: The impact of the LEAD program and new strategies of drug intervention in Seattle.* Unpublished honor thesis, Whitman College, Seattle, WA.

Belenko, S., Houser, K., & Welsh, W. (2012). *The Oxford handbook of sentencing and corrections.* New York, NY: Oxford University Press.

Blevins, K. R., Listwan, S. J., Cullen, F. T., & Jonson, C. L. (2010). A general strain theory of prison violence and misconduct: An integrated model of inmate behavior. *Journal of Contemporary Criminal Justice, 26*(2), 148–166.

Bonta, J. (2002). Offender risk assessment: Guidelines for selection and use. *Criminal Justice and Behavior, 29*(4), 355–379.

Bourdieu, P. (1990). *In other words: Essays towards a reflexive sociology.* Stanford University Press.

BJS - Bureau of Justice Statistics (2018). Prisoners in 2016. Summary, NCJ 251149. Office of Justice Programs, U.S. Department of Justice.

Cahalan, M. W., & Parsons, L. A. (1987). *Historical corrections statistics in the United States, 1850–1984.* US Department of Justice, Bureau of Justice Statistics.

Carson, E. A. (2015). Prisoners in 2014, Report: NCJ 248955, Office of Justice Programs, U.S. Department of Justice.

Carson, E. A. (2018). Prisoners in 2016, Report: NCJ 251149, Office of Justice Programs, U.S. Department of Justice.

Carson, E. A. & Anderson, E. (2016). Prisoners in 2015, Report: NCJ 250229, Office of Justice Programs, U.S. Department of Justice.

Clear, T. R., Reisig, M. D., & Cole, G. F. (2018). *American corrections.* Boston, MA: Cengage Learning.

Cochran, J. C. (2012). The ties that bind or the ties that break: Examining the relationship between visitation and prisoner misconduct. *Journal of Criminal Justice, 40*(5), 433–440.

Cowart, D. (2017). Transgender prisoners face sexual assault and discrimination at Pittsburgh jail. American Civil Liberties Union, https://www.aclu.org/.

Cunningham, M. D., & Sorensen, J. R. (2006). Actuarial models for assessing prison violence risk: Revisions and extensions of the risk assessment scale for prison (RASP). *Assessment, 13*(3), 253–265.

Davis, S., & Roswell, B. (Eds.). (2013). *Turning teaching inside out: A pedagogy of transformation for community-based education.* Springer.

Dewey, John. 1916. Democracy and Education: An Introduction to the Philosophy of Education. New York, NY: The MacMillan Company.

Draine, J., Salzer, M. S., Culhane, D. P., & Hadley, T. R. (2002). Role of social disadvantage in crime, joblessness, and homelessness among persons with serious mental illness. *Psychiatric Services, 53*(5), 565–573.

Entry, N. (2013). A National Survey of Criminal Justice Diversion Programs and Initiatives. Center for Health and Justice Alternatives at TASC, December.

Erisman, W., & Contardo, J. B. (2005). Learning to Reduce Recidivism: A 50-State Analysis of Postsecondary Correctional Education Policy. Institute for Higher Education Policy.

Fabelo, T., Thompson, M. D., Plotkin, M., Carmichael, D., Marchbanks, M. P., & Booth, E. A. (2011). *Breaking schools' rules: A statewide study of how school discipline relates to students' success and juvenile justice involvement.* New York: Council of State Governments Justice Center.

Flanagan, T. J. (1983). Correlates of institutional misconduct among state prisoners. *Criminology, 21*(1), 29–40.

Freire, Paulo. 1970. Pedagogia do Oprimido. Rio de Janeiro: Edições Paz e Terra.

Foucault, M. (1977). Discipline and Punish, trans. *Alan Sheridan (New York: Vintage, 1979), 242.*

Gaes, G. G., Wallace, S., Gilman, E., Klein-Saffran, J., & Suppa, S. (2002). The influence of prison gang affiliation on violence and other prison misconduct. *The Prison Journal*, *82*(3), 359–385.

Gendreau, P. (1996). Offender rehabilitation: What we know and what needs to be done. *Criminal Justice and Behavior*, *23*(1), 144–161.

Gendreau, P., Goggin, C. E., & Law, M. A. (1997). Predicting prison misconducts. *Criminal Justice and behavior*, *24*(4), 414–431.

Glaze, L. E., & Maruschak, L. M. (2008). *Parents in prison and their minor children*. Washington, DC: US Department of Justice, Office of Justice Programs.

Giallombardo, R. (1966). *Society of women: A study of a women's prison* (p. 204). New York, NY: Wiley.

Goffman, E. (1961). On the characteristics of total institutions. In *Symposium on preventive and social psychiatry* (pp. 43–84). Washington, DC: Walter Reed Army Medical Centre.

Goldstein, P. J. (1985). The drugs/violence nexus: A tripartite conceptual framework. *Journal of drug issues*, *15*(4), 493–506.

Gould, C., McGeorge, T., & Slade, K. (2017). Suicide screening tools for use in incarcerated offenders: A systematic review. *Archives of Suicide Research*, *22*(3), 345–364.

Griffin, M. L., & Hepburn, J. R. (2013). Inmate misconduct and the institutional capacity for control. *Criminal Justice and Behavior*, *40*(3), 270–288.

Hanser, R. D. (2013). *Community corrections*. Los Angeles, CA: Sage Publications.

Holtfreter, K., & Morash, M. (2003). The needs of women offenders. *Women & Criminal Justice*, *14*(2–3), 137–160.

Irwin, J., & Cressey, D. R. (1962). Thieves, convicts and the inmate culture. *Social Problems*, *10*(2), 142–155.

James, S. E., Herman, J. L., Rankin, S., Keisling, M., Mottet, L., & Anafi, M. (2016). The Report of the 2015 U.S. Transgender Survey. Washington, DC: National Center for Transgender Equality.

Jenness, V., & Fenstermaker, S. (2014). Agnes goes to prison: Gender authenticity, Transgender inmates in prisons for men, and pursuit of "The Real Deal." *Gender & Society*, *28*(1), 5–31.

Kigerl, A., & Hamilton, Z. (2016). The impact of transfers between prisons on inmate misconduct: Testing importation, deprivation, and transfer theory models. *The Prison Journal*, *96*(2), 232–257.

Kruttschnitt, C. (2010). The paradox of women's imprisonment. *Daedalus*, *139*(3), 32–42.

Harlow, C. W. (2003). Education and Correctional Populations. Bureau of Justice Statistics Special Report.

Lamb, H. R., & Weinberger, L. E. (2005). The shift of psychiatric inpatient care from hospitals to jails and prisons. *Journal of the American Academy of Psychiatry and the law Online*, *33*(4), 529–534.

Lahm, K. F. (2008). Inmate-On-Inmate Assault A Multilevel Examination of Prison Violence. *Criminal Justice and Behavior*, *35*(1), 120–137.

Langan, P. A., & Levin, D. J. (2002). Recidivism of prisoners released in 1994. *Federal Sentencing Reporter*, *15*(1), 58–65.

Lahm, K. F. (2009). Educational participation and inmate misconduct. *Journal of Offender Rehabilitation*, *48*(1), 37–52.

LeBlanc, M., & Loeber, R. (1998). Developmental criminology updated. *Crime and Justice, 23*, 115–198.

Lindsey, A. M., Mears, D. P., Cochran, J. C., Bales, W. D., & Stults, B. J. (2015). In prison and far from home spatial distance effects on inmate misconduct. *Crime & Delinquency*, DOI: 10.1177/0011128715614017.

Loeber, Farrington, Stouthamer-Loeber, Caspi, A., White, H. R., Wei, E. H., & Beyers, J. M. (2003). The development of male offending. Key findings from fourteen years of the Pittsburgh Youth Study. In T. Thornberry, & M. Krohn (Eds.), *Taking stock of delinquency. An overview of findings from contemporary longitudinal studies* (pp. 93–139). New York: Kluwer Academic/Plenum Publishers.

Maruschak, L. M., Berzofsky, M., & Unangst, J. (2015). *Medical problems of state and federal prisoners and jail inmates, 2011–12*. Washington, DC: US Department of Justice, Office of Justice Programs, Bureau of Justice Statistics.

MacKenzie, D. L. (2012). The effectiveness of corrections-based work and academic and vocational education programs. In J. Petersilia, & K. R. Reitz (Eds.), *The Oxford handbook of sentencing and corrections*. New York, NY: Oxford University Press.

Morris, R. G., & Worrall, J. L. (2014). Prison architecture and inmate misconduct a multilevel assessment. *Crime & Delinquency, 60*(7), 1083–1109.

Morash, M., Bynum, T. S., & Koons-Witt, B. (1998). *Women offenders: Programming needs and promising approaches*. Washington, DC: US Department of Justice, Office of Justice Programs, National Institute of Justice.

National PRA Resource Center (n.d.) PREA standards in focus. Available online https://www.prearesourcecenter.org/StandardsinFocus [last visited 05-29-2018].

Otis, M. (1913). A perversion not commonly noted. *The Journal of Abnormal Psychology, 8*(2), 113.

Owen, B. A. (1998). *In the mix: Struggle and survival in a women's prison*. SUNY Press.

Perry, A. E., Marandos, R., Coulton, S., & Johnson, M. (2010). Screening tools assessing risk of suicide and self-harm in adult offenders: A systematic review. *International journal of offender therapy and comparative criminology, 54*(5), 803–828.

Selling, L. S. (1931). The pseudo family. *American Journal of Sociology, 37*(2), 247–253.

Steiner, B., & Wooldredge, J. (2008). Inmate versus environmental effects on prison rule violations. *Criminal Justice and Behavior, 35*(4), 438–456.

Solinas-Saunders, M., & Stacer, M. J. (2012). Prison resources and physical/verbal assault in prison: A comparison of male and female inmates. *Victims & Offenders, 7*(3), 279–311.

Solinas-Saunders, M., Anderson, L., Huey, J., Ceesay, A., Ferrandino, J., Tsataros, D., & Tsolakos, J. (2017). Service learning in a regional Urban Midwest University: An overview of five projects. *Journal of the Indiana Academy of the Social Sciences, 16*(1), 10.

Solinas-Saunders, M., & Stacer, M. J. (2017). A retrospective analysis of repeated incarceration using a national sample: What makes female inmates different from male inmates? *Victims & Offenders, 12*(1), 138–173.

Sykes, G. (1958). *The society of captives Princeton*. NJ: Princeton University.

The Sentencing Project (1986). *Incarcerated Women and Girls*. Facts Sheet. Available at http://www.sentencingproject.org/wp-content/uploads/2016/02/Incarcerated-Women-and-Girls.pdf [last visited May 18-2018].

Steiner, B., & Wooldredge, J. (2009). Rethinking the link between institutional crowding and inmate misconduct. *The Prison Journal*, *89*(2), 205–233.

James, D. J., & Glaze, L. E. (2006). *Mental health problems of prison and jail inmates*. Washington, DC: US Department of Justice, Office of Justice Programs, Bureau of Justice Statistics.

Wagner, P., & Sawyer, W. (2018). Mass Incarceration: The Whole Pie 2018, Press Release, Prison Policy Initiative. Available at https://www.prisonpolicy.org/reports/pie2018.html (last visited on May 23, 2018).

Ward, D. A., & Kassebaum, G. G. (1966). *Women's prison: Sex and social structure*. Albany, NY: Transaction Publishers.

Welch, M. (2011). *Corrections: A critical approach*. New York, NY: Routledge, New York, NY.

CHAPTER 13

The Legal Protection of Inmates and the Death Penalty

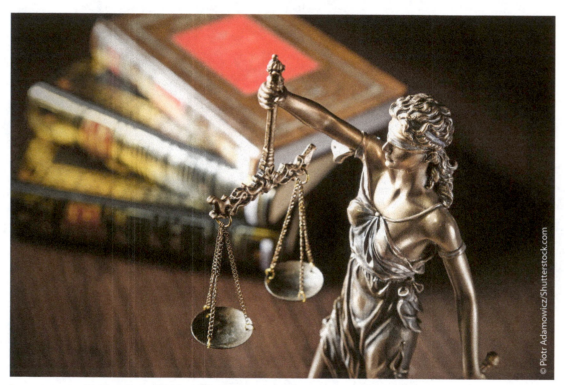

Law concept with Themis and books in background. Composition in court library

© Piotr Adamowicz/Shutterstock.com

LEARNING OBJECTIVES

- Discuss the principles that guide inmate litigation
- Articulate the main appeals available to U.S. inmates
- Provide examples of successful lawsuits protecting inmates' constitutional rights
- Provide an overview of the various laws that discipline the use of the death penalty in the United States
- Compare the arguments pro and against the death penalty

INTRODUCTION

This chapter focuses on the rights of offenders and the death penalty. While the two topics are not directly linked, one could argue that the controversies surrounding the use of the death penalty in the U.S. criminal justice system stem from the failure to observe the defendant's constitutional rights. Although it is often assumed that a criminal conviction wipes out an individual's constitutional rights, this assumption is far from real. Criminal defendants preserve their constitutional rights after a conviction and throughout their stay in institutions of corrections. Legal appeals in death penalty cases are usually the only opportunity the condemned has to change their path to execution. Perhaps the most relevant milestone in the determination of offenders' constitutional rights is *Wolff v. McDonnell* where the U.S. Supreme Court ruled that incarceration does not automatically erase the offenders' constitutional rights (1974).

INMATES' APPEALS

The mistreatment of prison inmates became a major concern during the civil rights' era. Many changes have been introduced since the inception of the movement named as "Prisoners' Rights' Movement." Today, criminal case defendants can continue to challenge the decision of the court even after their convictions by filing petitions through the Federal District Courts. Two main forms of appeal are commonly used by convicted prisoners: the writ of *habeas corpus* and the civil rights' claim. The writ of *habeas corpus* (latin for "having the body") is a petition through which prisoners can challenge the legality of incarceration. If a person was wrongly convicted because of procedural errors, prisoners have the right to file a petition to re-examine the case. The civil rights' claim, also known as Section 1983, provides the inmate with the opportunity to challenge the legality of the conditions of incarceration. By filing a civil rights' claim, inmates have the opportunity to argue that prison administrators are violating their constitutional rights by subjecting them to cruel and unusual punishment (prohibited under the Eighth Amendment of the U.S. Constitution). Bureau of Justice Statistics' estimate (Scalia, 2002) show that the number of petitions filed by state inmates peaked in the late 1990s with 68,235 petitions in 1996 alone. The number of petitions fell drastically after the 1996 Prison Litigation Reform Act which limited the right of inmates to file petitions (specifically petitions that challenged the legality of the conditions of their incarceration). The proponents of the Act meant to reduce the number of "frivolous" legal complaints that were seen as a disruption of the administrative practices of correctional institutions and give administrators an opportunity to remedy the problem without embarking in complicated legal appeal processes that would add to the already massive criminal courts' caseload (Prison Litigation Reform Act, 1996). Critics of the Act, point out that, when it comes to inmates' petitions, a frivolous petition is "simply one that does not raise a claim the courts are willing to entertain" (Herman, 2012: 263). While the idea that a legal process would provide prison administrations the opportunity to address the issue before embarking in expensive legal procedures might make sense, legal experts argue that this has created a backlog of cases that legitimately denounced inmates' sexual abuses at the hand of prison guards. Because the Act added several steps to the process by allowing prison administrations to weed cases out, for cases recognized as legitimate, the internal process often limits the expediency of the resolution of a case (Herman, 2012).

In prison, inmates preserve their constitutional rights and they have the right to free speech and practice religion (First Amendment). Inmates are also protected by the Fourth Amendment against unreasonable searches and seizures during confinement. The Eighth Amendment protects inmates from cruel and unusual punishment. Finally, the Fourteenth Amendment grants inmates due process which also includes internal hearings for cases of misconduct and violation of facility's rules. While inmates retain their constitutional rights during incarceration, their rights are more limited in scope than those of private citizens. This is due to the fact that inmates' right to exercise their freedom (as protected by the U.S. Constitution) can – at times – interfere with the normal functioning of the prison or threaten the safety of procedures that must be maintained at all times. In addition, inmates' exercise of constitutional rights might interfere with the mission of rehabilitation when it limits the execution of programs or prevents inmates from participating in such programs (Palmer & Palmer, 2004). Limitations of inmates' constitutional rights were specified in *Procunier v. Martinez* (1974) when the court ruled that the inmates' mail may be subjected to censorship to the extent necessary to maintain safety. Similarly, in *Turner v. Safley* (1987), the court ruled that mail that circulates from one inmate to another may be banned if "reasonably related to penological interests" (as cited in Clear et al., 2016: 107). In *Bell v. Wolfish* (1979), the court decided that strip searches may be carried out when the facility's need for such searches outweighs the personal rights invaded (Clear et al., 2016: 109). Another example is that of *O'Lone v. Estate of Shabazz* (1987) which clarified that the right to religious practices is not violated if inmates' work commitment makes it impossible to attend religious services. Corrections institutions have been successful in many cases of inmate litigations that challenged the ability of the institutions to maintain safety, implement a regimented routine, or provide rehabilitation services.

THE U.S. DEATH PENALTY

Since 1976, the United States executed 1,476 offenders, 16 of whom were women. The vast majority of executions were carried out in the Southern Region of the country. The year 1999 was the year with the largest number of executions (with 98 total executions) (DPIC, n.d.). While African Americans/blacks represent only 12.6% of the U.S. population (U.S. Census, 2010), they are overrepresented in every area of the criminal justice system, including the death penalty. More than 1/3 of all defendants sentenced to death were black. Currently, 41% of those on death row are black defendants (DPIC, n.d.). While 31 states currently retain the death penalty as a form of punishment, estimates indicate that the number of death sentences went from 295 in 1998 to 39 in 2017 (DPIC, n.d.). Table 13.1 from the Bureau of Justice Statistics reports the current situation with the death penalty in the United States.

Firing squad

Table 13.1 Status of the death penalty, December 31, 2016

Executions in 2016		Number of prisoners under sentence of death		Jurisdictions without death penalty
Georgia	9	California	742	Alaska
Texas	7	Florida	382	Connecticut
Alabama	2	Texas	244	District of Columbia
Florida	1	Alabama	183	Hawaii
Missouri	1	Pennsylvania	174	Illinois
		North Carolina	150	Iowa
		Ohio	140	Maine
		Arizona	118	Maryland
		Nevada	83	Massachusetts
		Louisiana	73	Michigan
		Tennessee	63	Minnesota
		Georgia	58	New Jersey
		Federal Bureau of Prisons	58	North Dakota
		Mississippi	47	Rhode Island
		Oklahoma	46	Vermont
		18 other jurisdictions*	253	West Virginia
				Wisconsin
Total	20	Total	2,814	

*New Mexico repealed the death penalty for offenses committed on or after July 1, 2009.

As of December 31, 2016, two males in New Mexico were under previously imposed death sentences.

Source: Bureau of Justice Statistics, National Prisoner Statistics program (NPS-8), 2016.

THE SUPREME COURT OF THE UNITED STATES AND THE DEALTH PENALTY

The U.S. Supreme Court has intervened many times to rule over the controversies around the death penalty. Among the most cited cases are (in chronological order):

1972   *Furman v. Georgia* (408 U.S. 238): temporarily invalidated of the use of capital punishment in the United States due to the verified arbitrariness of procedures which made the use of the death penalty unconstitutional. Since Furman, states have adopted the bi-furcated hearing procedures, through which the verdict and the death sentence are argued in separate hearings.

1976   *Gregg v. Georgia* (428 U.S. 153): reinstated of the use of capital punishment in the United States. The ruling provided an opportunity to use guided discretion in the assessment of "aggravating" and "mitigating" factors in death penalty cases.

1977   *Coker v. Georgia* (433 U.S. 584): invalidated the death penalty for rape.

2002   *Atkins v. Virginia* (536 U.S. 304): excluded individuals with mental disabilities from capital sentences; however, no guidance was provided to states for the assessment of the defendant's mental incompetence at trial.

2005   *Roper v. Simmons* (543 U.S. 551): invalidated the death penalty for juveniles.

2008   *Kennedy v. Louisiana* (554 U.S. 407): invalidated the death penalty for all other crimes other than pre-meditated murder (first-degree murder).

CONTROVERSIES SURROUNDING THE APPLICATION OF THE DEATH PENALTY IN THE US

Scientists have argued that regardless of ideologies, evidence suggests that the application of the death penalty tends to be controversial because of the fallacies we have experienced throughout its history (Steiker & Steiker, 2012; Welch, 2011).

One of the main concerns about the application of the death penalty is that the arbitrariness used in death penalty cases has caused significant racial disparities. Perhaps one of the most influential studies on racial disparities in death penalty cases is the study developed by Baldus, Pulaski, & Woodworth (1983) that examined 2,000 murder cases in the state of Georgia. The study found that defendants charged with the murder of a white person were 4.3 times more likely to be sentenced to death than those charged with the death of a black person. Black defendants charged with the murder of a white victim were at the highest risk for receiving the death penalty. The findings in Baldus, Pulaski, and

Woodworth (1983) were then replicated with a sample of Pennsylvania's defendants (Baldus, Woodworth, Zuckerman, & Weiner, 1997). The research findings in these two studies were consistent with those that Wolfgan published in the 1970s after analyzing data on rape defendants. Wolfgan and Riedel (1975) found that black defendants convicted of raping a white victim had more than 30% chance to be sentenced to death when compared to defendants in the other racial groups. While research evidence confirms that racial discrimination represents one of the main fallacies of the death penalty, the U.S. Supreme Court ruled that such evidence does not indicate that racial discrimination is purposefully used in death penalty cases (*McCleskey v. Kemp*, 1987).

Scientists argue that one of the main issues weakening the fairness of U.S. death penalty laws is inadequate representation. Steiker & Steiker (2012) point out that the main problem is that the majority of prosecutors in the United States are elected rather than appointed. When voters are concerned with crime and believe in the deterrent effect of capital punishment, an elected prosecutor seeking re-election might have a personal interest in pushing for capital punishment charges. It seems intuitive that, in jurisdictions where prosecutors are associated with the local politics, the politicization of the death penalty might contribute to weaken its fairness.

The high costs associated with bi-furcated hearings, lengthy appeals, and specialized counsel make the death penalty a very complicated business for constantly shrinking state budgets (Paternoster, 1991; Steiker & Steiker, 2012). One of the main concerns is that, faced with huge financial constraints, states attempts to take shortcuts in the training of death penalty counsels or acquisition of appropriate instruments to guarantee the integral preservation of evidence (especially biological evidence such as DNA samples). Although specific guidelines were introduced in 1989 (also revised in 2003) (see American Bar Association, 2003), studies show that the vast majority of states were found non-compliant (Steiker & Steiker, 2011). In addition, even when specific guidelines are employed, scientists argue the law cannot clearly distinguish between cases that are deserving of the death penalty and cases that are not, leading to a big deal of discretionary power used by all individuals involved throughout the prosecutorial and trial processes (Zimring & Johnson, 2011). Such discretionary power is also evident throughout the process Governors follow to pardon those wrongfully convicted (Welch, 2011).

One of the main concerns about the application of the death penalty in the United States pertains to the erroneous conviction of innocent individuals (Steiker & Steiker, 2012; Welch, 2011). When specific guidelines for the accuracy of information shared between defendants and their counselors are not observed and when the evidence from criminal investigations is not properly stored or used, there is always the risk that an innocent person might end up on death row becoming a victim of the criminal justice system. While this might sound hypothetical to the reader, the number of wrongful convictions in the United States is not irrelevant. The special issue in this section focuses on the problem of wrongful convictions.

The next two pages provide an overview of the history of the death penalty in Indiana. The document is available via the Indiana Department of Correction.

History of Capital Punishment in Indiana

Capital punishment has been a part of Indiana's criminal justice system since early in the state's history. Between 1897 and 2009, a total of 92 men have been executed in the State of Indiana for capital offenses. Two offenders with death sentences in Indiana have been executed in another state; Michael Lee Lockhart was executed on December 9, 1997 in Texas and Alton Colman on April 26, 2002 in Ohio. On December 13, 1938, James Dalhover, a federal prisoner was executed at the Indiana State Prison.

Indiana State Prison/Death Chamber

In 1822, the first state prison was built in Jeffersonville, IN. In 1858, the state was looking for a second location to build another prison. Chancy Blair, a Michigan City business man who owned 102 acres of land on the western edge of the city limits, offered to sell his property to the state for the sum of $4,500. After purchasing the land and gaining financial support from the state legislature, construction began on the prison with 100 offenders being transferred from Jeffersonville. Both prisons in Michigan City and Jeffersonville were named the Indiana State Prison, one designated Prison North and the other Prison South. In 1922, Prison South was destroyed by a fire and the designation was no longer necessary.

The Death Chamber and Death Row are located at the Indiana State Prison (ISP) in Michigan City, IN. All executions since 1987 have taken place at ISP.

Execution by Hanging

Indiana's capital punishment statute originally became law in 1897. Between 1897 and 1913, hanging was the form of capital punishment and 13 individuals were executed by hanging. The last person to be executed by hanging was in 1907.

Execution by Electrocution

Electrocution as the prescribed method of execution was passed into law in 1913. The first electrocution of a condemned prisoner occurred Feb. 20, 1914, 11 months after the legislation was adopted.

- Between 1914 and 1995, electrocution was used and 62 executed by electrocution.

- On December 8, 1994, Gregory Resnover was put to death in the electric chair. This was the first electrocution since 1985. He was the last offender to be executed in the electric chair at the state prison.

- The last person executed before the moratorium on the death penalty in 1972 was Richard Kiefer, Allen County. He was executed on June 15, 1961.

Death Penalty Suspended

In 1972 the United States Supreme Court held that the death penalty as administered violated the United States Constitution Eighth Amendment prohibition against cruel and unusual punishment. A majority of the court found that the sentencing authority was not adequately guided in its discretion when imposing the death penalty, resulting in the death penalty being meted out in "arbitrary and capricious" ways. The Supreme Court's decision in Furman v. Georgia did not rule the death penalty itself to be unconstitutional, only the specific laws by which it was applied. Thus, the states quickly began to write new death penalty laws designed to comply with the court's ruling.

- In 1972, the U.S. Supreme Court in Furman v. Georgia held all state death penalty sentencing statutes were unconstitutional. As a result, seven men on Indiana's death row at the time had all of their sentences reduced to life in prison.

- In 1973, the Indiana General Assembly enacted a new death penalty sentencing statute to replace the statute struck down by the U.S. Supreme Court in Furman.

- In 1977, the Indiana Supreme Court struck down Indiana's 1973 death penalty sentencing statute based on the U.S. Supreme Court decision in Woodson v. North Carolina. The death sentences of the eight men on Indiana's death row were set aside.

- On October 1, 1977, a new Indiana death penalty sentencing statute, modeled on statutes upheld by U.S. Supreme Court, took effect. It remains in effect today.

Execution by Lethal Injection

In 1995, the Indiana Legislature passed, and the governor signed, a law making lethal injection the method of execution in Indiana.

- Since 1995, 19 individuals have been executed by lethal injection.

- The first execution by lethal injection in Indiana occurred on July 18, 1996, when Tommie J. Smith, convicted in 1981 of murder in Marion County, was executed.

- On December 11, 2009, Offender Matthew Eric Wrinkles was the last offender to be executed.

Current execution procedure is found in Indiana Code 35-38-6 and requires that the lethal injection execution take place inside the walls of the Indiana State Prison at Michigan City before sunrise.

> **IC 35-38-6-1 Execution Procedure**
> (a) The punishment of death shall be inflicted by intravenous injection of a lethal substance or substances into the convicted person:
> (1) in a quantity sufficient to cause the death of the convicted person; and
> (2) until the convicted person is dead.
> (b) The death penalty shall be inflicted before the hour of sunrise on a date fixed by the sentencing court. However, the execution must not occur until at least one hundred (100) days after the conviction.
> (c) The superintendent of the state prison, or persons designated by the superintendent, shall designate the person who is to serve as the executioner.
> (d) The department of correction may adopt rules under IC 4-22-2 necessary to implement subsection(a). [As added by P.L.311-1983, SEC.3. Amended by P.L.294-1995, SEC.1; P.L.20-2002, SEC.1.]

LEARNING EXERCISES

The following cases dealt with the violation of inmates' constitutional rights:

1. *Procunier v. Martinez* (1974)
2. *Turner v. Saftley* (1987)
3. *Bell v. Wolfish* (1979)

Based on your understanding of the cases, how did the institution infringe on prisoners' rights? How did the court explain that violations did not occur?

BIBLIOGRAPHY

American Bar Association. (2003). ABA Guidelines for the Appointment and Performance of Defense Counsel in Death Penalty Cases. *Hofstra Law Review, 31*(4), 2.

Atkins v. Virginia, (2002). 536 U.S. 304, 122 S. Ct. 2242, 153 L. Ed. 2d 335.

Baldus, D. C., Pulaski, C., & Woodworth, G. (1983). Comparative review of death sentences: An empirical study of the Georgia experience. *The Journal of Criminal Law and Criminology (1973–), 74*(3), 661–753.

Baldus, D. C., Woodworth, G., Zuckerman, D., & Weiner, N. A. (1997). Racial discrimination and the death penalty in the post-Furman era: An empirical and legal overview with recent findings from Philadelphia. *Cornell Law Review, 83*, 1638.

Bell v. Wolfish (1979). 441 U.S. 520, 99 S. Ct. 1861, 60 L. Ed. 2d 447.

Coker v. Georgia (1977). 433 U.S. 584, 97 S. Ct. 2861, 53 L. Ed. 2d 982.

Davis, E., & Snell, T.L. (2018). Capital Punishment, 2016. Bureau of Justice Statistics, Office of Justice Programs, U.S. Department of Justice, NCJ 251430.

Death Penalty Information Center (n.d.). Facts about the death penalty. Available at https://deathpenaltyinfo.org/documents/FactSheet.pdf [last visited 5-27-2018].

United States Census (2010). Community facts. Available at https://factfinder.census.gov/faces/tableservices/jsf/pages/productview.xhtml?src=CF [last visited 5-27-2018].

Kennedy v. Louisiana (2008). 554 U.S. 407, 128 S. Ct. 2641, 171 L. Ed. 2d 525.

Furman v. Georgia (1972). 408 U.S. 238, 92 S. Ct. 2726, 33 L. Ed. 2d 346.

Gregg v. Georgia (1976). 428 U.S. 153, 96 S. Ct. 2909, 49 L. Ed. 2d 859.

Herman, S. N. (2012). Prison litigation reform acts. *Federal Sentencing Reporter, 24*(4), 263–267.

McCleskey v. Kemp (1987). 481 U.S. 279, 107 S. Ct. 1756, 95 L. Ed. 2d 262.

O'Lone v. Estate of Shabazz (1987). 482 U.S. 342, 107 S. Ct. 2400, 96 L. Ed. 2d 282.

Palmer, J. W., & Palmer, S. E. (2004). *Constitutional Rights of Prisoners* (7th ed.), Cincinnati, OH: Anderson Publishing Co.

Prison Litigation Reform Act (1996). 104–134, §§ 801–10, 110 Stat. 1321.

Procunier v. Martinez (1974). 416 U.S. 396, 94 S. Ct. 1800, 40 L. Ed. 2d 224.

Roper v. Simmons (2005). 543 U.S. 551, 125 S. Ct. 1183, 161 L. Ed. 2d 1.

Scalia, J. (2002). *Prisoner Petitions Filed in US District Courts, 2000: With Trends 1980–2000*. US Department of Justice, Office of Justice Programs, Bureau of Justice Statistics.

Steiker, C. S., & Steiker, J. M. (2012). Broken and beyond repair: The American death penalty and the insuperable obstacles to reform. In J. Petersilia, & K. R. Reitz (Eds.), *The Oxford handbook of sentencing and corrections*. New York, NY: Oxford University Press.

Turner v. Safley (1987). 482 U.S. 78, 107 S. Ct. 2254, 96 L. Ed. 2d 64.

Zimring, F. E., & Johnson, D. T. (2011). *The dark at the top of the stairs: Four destructive influences of capital punishment on American criminal justice*. New York, NY: Oxford University Press.

Welch, M. (2011). *Corrections: A critical approach*. New York, NY: Routledge, New York, NY.

Wolfgang, M. E., & Riedel, M. (1975). Rape, race, and the death penalty in Georgia. *American Journal of Orthopsychiatry, 45*(4), 658.

Wrongful Convictions, Exonerations, and the National Registry of Exonerations

The words Wrongful Conviction concept and theme written in vintage wooden letterpress type on a grunge background

Wrongful convictions are convictions in which defendants have been erroneously charged and convicted of criminal acts they did not commit or that never happened. They represent an indelible stain on the U.S. criminal justice system in that they contribute to the creation of new victims of the state on any given day (Weigand, 2008). The exact rate of wrongful convictions in the United States is not known, however, estimates show that, for cases that involved sexual assault, wrongful convictions occur at a rate of 11.6% (Walsh, Hussemann, Flynn, Yahner, &

Golian, 2017). While exonerations post convictions are possible through a system of appeals that we have explored in Section V, most exonerations actually materialize many years after a defendant was convicted or incarcerated. Between 1989 and 2018, there were 2,224 documented exonerations in the United States. Data on exonerations is collected by the National Registry of Exonerations. Founded in 2012 as result of a collaboration among the Newkirk Center for Science and Society at the University of California, Irvine, the University of Michigan Law School, and Michigan State University College of Law, the National Registry of Exonerations was created in association with the Center on Wrongful Convictions at Northwestern University School of Law. The Registry defines exonerations as "cases in which a person was wrongly convicted of a crime and later cleared of all the charges based on new evidence of innocence" (The National Registry of Exoneration, n.d.).

Women represent 8% of all criminal defendants exonerated for a crime that they did not commit. Almost two thirds of the women exonerees (63%) were convicted for crimes that never actually happened. This proportion is three times as high as the rate for men (21%). In addition, 40% of female exonerees were charged with crimes against children, compared with 22% of men exonerees (Jackson & Gross, 2014).

An analysis by race confirms the trend that sees Black defendants overrepresented in every area of the criminal justice system. As of October 2016, Blacks were 47% of all exonerees. More specifically, blacks exonerated for crimes they did not commit represented 50% of all exonerees in murder cases, 59% of those exonerated in sexual assault cases, 25% of exonerees in child sexual abuse cases, 62% of exonerees in robbery cases, and 55% of exonerees in drug offense cases.Misconduct by police was 22% more likely to occur in cases of black defendants than white defendants (Gross, Possley, & Stephens, 2017).

Misconduct by police authorities is only one of the reasons leading to erroneous convictions. Other common problems leading to wrongful convictions include incompetent legal counsel, failure to preserve DNA evidence, prosecutorial misconduct, erroneous witness testimony or false identification, police forced interrogation, false confession, and guilty plea.

Jackson & Gross (2016) estimated that 35% of all the cases of exonerations filed between 1989 and 2014 involved eye-witness mis-identification (509 cases out of 1,446). Among them, 17% were cases in which witnesses described crimes that never occurred.

A rigorous scientific study found that eye witness identification procedures can lead to false accusation in that reliance on one's memory can be very limiting. Scientists at the National Research Council reported that:

"[…] we have found that many factors influence the visual perceptual experience: dim illumination and brief viewing times, large viewing distances, duress, elevated emotions, and the presence of a visual distracting element such as a gun or knife. Gaps in sensory input are filled by expectations that are based on prior experiences with the world. Prior experiences are capable of biasing the visual perceptual experience and reinforcing an individual's conception of what was seen. We also have learned that these qualified perceptual experiences are stored by a system of memory that is highly malleable and continuously evolving, neither retaining nor divulging content in an informational vacuum. The fidelity of our memories to actual events may be compromised by many factors at all stages of processing, from uncoding to storage to retrieval. Unknown to the individual, memories are forgotten, reconstructed, updated, and distorted. Therefore, caution must be exercised when utilizing eyewitness procedures and when relying on eyewitness identifications in a judicial context." (2015: 1–2).

An analysis of the data on exonerations revealed that 12% of exonerations were cases of wrongful convictions based on false confessions (Gross & Possely, 2016). A breakdown by age and mental health status indicated that 70% of those who falsely confessed a crime they did not commit suffered from either a reported mental illness or intellectual disability. In addition, the analysis also showed that 38% of defendants who falsely confessed were under the age of 18 when the incident occurred (Gross & Possely, 2016). According to Drizin & Leo (2003), the main explanation to justify false confessions by defendants concerns police interrogation technique that tend to trick, confuse, or deceive suspects under interrogation. Some defendants are more susceptible to the influence of these techniques because of personality traits or mental health conditions (Leo, 2009). The Frontline documentary "The Confessions" portrays a complicated case of wrongful convictions based on the evidence produced through police forced confessions. The case featured four defendants (known to the public as the "Norfolk four"), Joseph Dick, Danial Williams, Eric Wilson, and Derek Dice, all veterans of the U.S. Navy. The four young men were charged for the rape and murder of an 18-year-old woman later sentenced for crimes they never committed (Bikel, 2010). The four men were pardoned by the Governor of Virginia in 2017 (Burstein, 2017).

The problem of wrongful convictions is especially troubling for cases that involve the death penalty or the threat that the death penalty will be on the table (as in the case of the "Norfolk four"). While one would expect more rigor in cases that involve first degree murder, the pressure that police department face to lock up the culprit and the complexity of the investigation may contribute to procedural errors. In a study that involved the examination of 5,760 capital cases filed between 1973 and 1995, Liebman, Fagan, West, and Lloyd (1999), found errors in 7 out of 10 cases. Research on wrongful convictions is needed. Focusing only on cases of exoneration can be misleading as they might represent a small fraction of all wrongful convictions.

BIBLIOGRAPHY

Bikel, O. (2010). The Confessions. PBS, Frontline. Available online https://www.pbs.org/wgbh/pages/frontline/the-confessions/ [last visited 05-29-2018].

Burstein, L. (2017). Breaking: Virginia Governor grants full pardons to the "Norfolk four," March 21. Available at http://www.norfolkfour.com/images/uploads/pdf_files/N4_Clemency_Press_Release.pdf [last visited 05-29-2018].

Drizin, S. A., & Leo, R. A. (2003). The problem of false confessions in the post-DNA world. *North Carolina Law Review*, *82*, 891.

Gross, S., Possley, M. & Stephens, K. (2017). Race and wrongful convictions in the United States. The National Registry of Exonerations. Available at http://www.law.umich.edu/special/exoneration/Documents/Race_and_Wrongful_Convictions.pdf [last visited 05-29-2018].

Gross, S., & Possley, M. (2016). For 50 years you've had the right to remain silent. So why do so many suspects confess to crimes they didn't commit? The Marshall Project, filed 06-12-2016.

Jackson, K. & Gross, S. (2014). Female exonerees: Trends and patterns. National Registry of Exonerations. Available a http://www.law.umich.edu/special/exoneration/Pages/Features.Female. Exonerees.aspx [last visited 05-29-2018].

Liebman, J. S., Fagan, J., West, V., & Lloyd, J. (1999). Capital attrition: Error rates in capital cases, 1973–1995. *Texas Law Review*, *78*, 1839.

Leo, R. A. (2009). False confessions: Causes, consequences and implications. *Journal of the American Academy of Psychiatry and the Law* 37: 332– 43.

National Registry of Exonerations. (2015). Guilty pleas and false confessions. Available at http://www.law.umich.edu/special/exoneration/Documents/NRE.Guilty.Plea.Article4.pdf [last retrieved 05-29-2018].

National Registry of Exonerations (n.d.). Information captured from the home page of the website.

National Research Council. (2015). *Identifying the culprit: Assessing eyewitness identification*. Washington, DC: National Academies Press.

Walsh, K., Hussemann, J., Flynn, A., Yahner, J., & Golian, L. (2017). Estimating the Prevalence of Wrongful Convictions. National Criminal Justice Reference Service, Office of Justice Programs, Document no. 251115.

Weigand, H. (2008). Rebuilding a life: The wrongfully convicted and exonerated. *Boston University Public Interest Law Journal*, *18*, 427.

Section VI

Offender Reentry

Criminal background check application form with glasses and ballpoint pen.

CHAPTER 14

Parole and Reintegration into Society

Feeling of joy. Receiving freedom after long imprisonment. The way out of prison.

LEARNING OBJECTIVES

- Discuss the main challenges ex-offenders face upon release

- Articulate the various instruments used in the U.S. criminal justice system to facilitate reentry

- Elaborate on the application of current policies to reduce the collateral damage of incarceration

INTRODUCTION

Knowledge of the field of corrections must include an understanding of the controversies surrounding ex-offender reentry. As Travis points out, almost all those incarcerated will return home at some point (2005). The majority of offenders released from prison will go back to the community where they came from; often struggling with the same challenges that led to their incarceration in the first place. Adding to the concerns of returning to communities ill equipped to help ex-felons re-integrate, are the challenges associated with the stigma of incarceration. The same terms "ex-felon," or "ex-offender" all redefine the individual based on the moment of separation from society (Goffman, 1968). On the other hand, we are prone to consider crime and deviance as destabilizing and unsustainable; for this reasons, we label those responsible as deviant (or criminal) (Becker, 2008).

Criminologists have manifested serious concerns over the re-integration of ex-offenders in society (Petersilia, 2003; Travis, 2002). On the other hand, the number of people churning in and out of prison is high and recidivism rates are above 40% (Durose, Cooper, & Snyder, 2014). A contemporary approach to reintegration focuses on the idea of helping offenders learn how to live independently in society, an effort that must begin on day one of their incarceration (La Vigne, Davies, Palmer & Halberstadt, 2008).

The idea of helping ex-offenders re-integrate into the community in not new to criminologists. Within the history of ex-offender reentry, the practice of releasing offenders on parole is of particular relevance.

PAROLE THROUGH HISTORY

Parole, from the French "*parole d'honneur*" (or word of honor, in English), literally means releasing a prisoner or an offender after he/she gave his word not to engage in further wrongdoing. The Bureau of Justice Statistics defines parole as "[..] a period of conditional supervised release in the community following a prison term. It includes parolees released through discretionary or mandatory supervised release from prison, those released from prison, those released through other types of post-custody conditional supervision, and those sentenced to a term of supervised release" (Kaeble & Glaze, 2017: 2).

In Medieval Europe, a knight defeated in combat was sometimes given another chance to survive if he promised (by giving his word of honor) to leave the battlefield (Mays & Winfree, 2014). After 1617, when the transportation of British convicts to the colonies began, parole was established as a system necessary to monitor the offenders. After serving a sentence, felons would become indentured servants continuing to provide cheap labor in exchange for food, clothing, and accommodation (Welch, 2013). In 1840, Superintendent Alexander Maconochie was assigned the penal colony in Norfolk Island (Australia). During his tenure, Maconochie observed that with a system of rewards (based on earning credits for early release), offenders were more likely to observe rules. Maconochie is often considered the father of parole in that he created the idea that a sentence can be reduced based on good behavior (Welch, 2013).

Maconochie is today also recognized as the first correctional expert to introduce the idea of indeterminate sentences. He believed that determinate sentences that did not provide an opportunity for early release were unfair. During his years at Norfolk, Maconochie observed that when offenders are rewarded for good behavior and are granted early release based on good conduct and hard labor, they are more likely to be rehabilitated prior to their release. Maconochie was dismissed after four years at Norfolk because others interpreted his innovative methods as "coddling of inmates." Maconochie also rejected the idea of corporal punishment, an old practice to which Norfolk went back soon after his departure (Welch, 2013).

In 1853, the English Parliament enacted the Penal Servitude Act to legally permit the release of prisoners under the supervision of police authorities (Mays & Winfree, 2014). In 1854, Sir Walter Crofton used Maconochie's reward system when appointed to the Irish prison system. According to a review by Welch (2013), Crofton's approach followed four separate stages during a felon's sentence:

Stage 1: Solitary confinement

Stage 2: Work assignment inside the prison

Stage 3: Reward for inmates with more liberty within the facility, based on the "ticket of leave" model designed by Maconochie.

Stage 4: Inmates earned the opportunity to be released back into the community.

In 1863, the medieval practice of early release became part of the Lieber Code to rule over the Civil War. The law recognized the possibility for soldiers captured during a battle to save themselves by promising not to further engage in the conflict (Mays & Winfree, 2014). Because the Lieber Code was recognized as International Law, this practice became known in other countries as well. Later, parole was recognized by the Hague Convention, becoming formal law of war also in Europe (Morris, 1997).

In 1876, the first formalized parole system was established within the Elmira Reformatory by Superintendent Zebulon R. Brockway (Welch, 2013). Although, some point out that "good time laws" were already part of the New York State statute since 1817 (Mays & Winfree, 2014). While Brockway advocated for proving juvenile offenders with the opportunity of early release upon demonstration of rehabilitation, several states passed legislation that granted parole to adult offenders as well (Illinois, Michigan, Pennsylvania, and Massachusetts were the first states to do so). By 1944, all states had passed legislation to include parole (Welch, 2013).

The state of New York was the first to introduce parole and define the conditions of community supervision. Although the Elmira reformatory was the first institution to formally adopt parole, no paid professional occupation was available to guarantee the supervision of those released on parole. Until 1845, the supervision of parolees in the community was assigned to "guardians" (volunteer citizens). In 1845, Massachusetts became the first state to create the parole officer position, a civil servant of the state (Mays & Winfree, 2014). In 1910, parole was formally introduced as part of the federal system (Mays & Winfree, 2014).

Central to the idea of "ticket to leave" under Maconochie was inmate labor. Offenders under the supervision of Maconochie gained skills and maintained labor, demonstrating an ability to provide for themselves under strict correctional rules. The focus on labor and employment continued to make parole a successful tool of the criminal justice system. Because most offenders were indigent, and often lacked the necessary skills to carry forward a trade, parole provided offenders with the opportunity to learn through employment (Welch, 2013).

Between the two world wars, during the Great Depression of the 1920s and 1930s, the use of parole became common practice in the United States, to alleviate the problem of overcrowding in both the state and federal correctional systems (Mays & Winfree, 2014). The number of inmates during those years went up from 74 inmates per 100,000 residents to 125 inmates per 100,000 residents (Mays & Winfree, 2014).

In 1930, the Bureau of Prison was created to supervise the federal prison system. In addition, a single parole board for the federal system was appointed to rule over federal parole cases. The board was comprised of eight experts directly appointed by the U.S. President and reported to the U.S. Attorney General. Many changes occurred over the years to allow for a more systematic control of an increasing number of cases across the United States. In the 1970s, the board was restructured into five different regions, each with a board member while the remaining members continued their appointment in Washington D.C. at the national headquarter. The decline in job opportunities for in industrial/manufacturing jobs that characterized much of the post-war era of the 20th century caused the parole system to shift focus from employment to treatment. With Martinson's "nothing works" conclusion of the 1970s (Martinson, 1974), the treatment approach was quickly condemned and boycotted for its inability to show changes in rehabilitation rates. Within less than 50 years, the U.S. criminal justice system transitioned from a philosophy of rehabilitation to a simplistic and mechanical focus on custody, management, and surveillance (Welch, 2013).

In 1984, Congress passed the Comprehensive Crime Control Act, which created the Sentencing Commission to rule over the newly introduced determinate sentencing system, *de facto* eliminating the possibility of parole in the federal prison system for all those convicted of a crime under federal court of law after November 1, 1987. However, federal inmates can still be granted early release based on good behavior (Mays & Winfree, 2014).

CONTEMPORARY PAROLE IN THE UNITED STATES

In addition to the federal government, by 2002, 16 states abolished parole boards, leading to a system where release is ruled in different ways across the nation. Clear, Reisig, & Cole (2014), highlight four different types of release in the U.S. correctional system:

- *Discretionary release*, conditional supervision decided by a parole board according to the state's guidelines.
- *Mandatory release*, after the completion of a certain portion of a sentence, based on state laws or parole guidelines.
- *Probation release*, after a period of incarceration under the condition identified by a judge.
- *Other conditional release*, by using other agencies in the community, such as half way houses, or work release programs.
- *Expiration release*, for offenders who maxed on their sentence minus good conduct and cannot be sent back to prison.

Some states, however, use a combination of methods (Mays & Winfree, 2014).

PAROLE BY THE NUMBERS

By the end of 2015, the parole population in the United States was 870,500, recording an increase of 12,800 offenders since 2014. In 2015, 1 every 285 adult residents in the United States was under parole supervision. Exits from parole also increased in 2015, with a total number of 463,700 offenders, of whom 14% returned to incarceration (Kaeble & Bonczar, 2017).

Figure 14.1 Adults on parole at yearend, 2005–2015

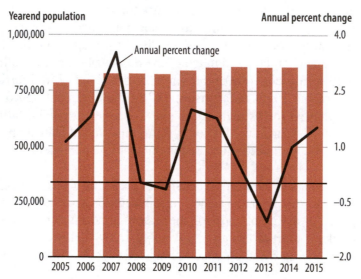

Note: Estimates are based on most recent data and may differ from previously published statistics. See *Methodology.*

Source: Bureau of Justice Statistics, Annual Parole Survey, 2005–2015.

Table 14.1 Adults under community supervision on probation or parole, yearend 2005–2015

Year	Total	Probation	Parole
2005	4,946,600	4,162,300	784,400
2006	5,035,000	4,236,800	798,200
2007	5,119,000	4,293,000	826,100
2008	5,093,400	4,271,200	826,100
2009	5,019,900	4,199,800	824,600
2010	4,888,500	4,055,900	840,800
2011	4,818,300	3,973,800	855,500
2012	4,790,700	3,944,900	858,400
2013	4,749,800	3,912,900	849,500
2014	4,713,200	3,868,400	857,700
2015	4,650,900	3,789,800	870,500
Percent change, 2005–2015	−6.0%	−8.9%	11.0%
Percent change, 2014–2015	−1.3%	−2.0%	1.5%

Note: Counts are rounded to the nearest 100. Detail may not sum to total due to rounding. Estimates are based on most recent data and may differ from previously published statistics. Reporting methods for some probation agencies changed over time. *See Methodology.*

Source: Bureau of Justice Statistics, Annual Probation Survey and Annual Parole Survey, 2005–2015.

A major spike in the number of offenders placed on parole occurred in 2007 when a total number of 826,100 parolees were reported by the Bureau of Justice Statistics, a significant increase from the 798,200 count of the previous year (Kaeble & Bonczar, 2017).

Table 14.2 Rate of parole exits, by type of exit, 2005 and 2010–2015

Type of exit	2005	2010	2011	2012	2013[d]	2014[d]	2015[d]
Total exit rate[a]	66	67	63	58	54	53	54
Completion	30	35	34	34	32	33	33
Returned to incarceration	25	23	20	15	14	14	14
With new sentence	8	6	6	5	4	4	4
With revocation	16	16	13	8	9	8	8
Other/unknown	1	1	2	1	1	1	2
Absconder	7	6	6	6	4	3	4
Other unsatisfactory[b]	1	1	1	1	1	1	1
Transferred to another state	1	1	1	1	0	0	0
Death	1	1	1	1	1	1	1
Other[c]	1	1	1	1	1	1	2

Note: Detail may not sum to total due to rounding.

[a]The ratio of the number of parolees exiting supevision during the year to the average daily parole population (i.e., average of the January 1 and December 31 populations within the reporting year).

[b]Includes parolees discharged from supervision who failed to meet all conditions of supervision, including some who had their parole sentence revoked but were not incarcerated because their sentence was immediately reinstated, and other types of unsatisfactory exits. Includes some early terminations and expirations of sentence reported as unsatisfactory exits.

[c]Includes, but not limited to, parolees discharged from supervision because they were deported or transferred to the jurisdiction of Immigration and Customs Enforcement, had their sentence terminated by the court through an appeal, and were transferred to another state through an interstate compact agreement or discharged to probation supervision.

[d]Includes imputed data for California, based on information provided for 2012.

Source: Bureau of Justice Statistics, Annual Parole Survey, 2005 and 2010–2015.

Table 14.3 Characteristics of adults on parole, 2005, 2014, and 2015

Characteristic	2005	2014	2015
Sex	100%	100%	100%
Male	88	88	87
Female	12	12	13
Race/Hispanic origin[a]	100%	100%	100%
White	41	43	44
Black/African American	40	39	38
Hispanic/Latino	18	16	16
American Indian/Alaska Native	1	1	1
Asian/Native Hawaiian/Other Pacific Islander	1	1	1
Two or more races	0	--	--
Status of supervision	100%	100%	100%
Active	83	84	83
Inactive	4	5	5
Absconder	7	6	6
Supervised out of state	4	4	4
Financial conditions remaining	...	0	0
Other	2	2	3
Maximum sentence to incarceration	100%	100%	100%
Less than 1 year	3	6	6
1 year or more	97	94	94
Most serious offense	100%	100%	100%
Violent	26%	31%	32%
Sex offense	...	7	8
Other violent	...	24	24
Property	24%	22%	21%
Drug	37%	31%	31%
Weapon	...	4%	4%
Other[b]	13%	12%	13%

Note: Detail may not sum to total due to rounding. Estimates based on most recent data and may differ from previously published statistics. See Methodology. Characteristics based on parolees with known type of status.

-- Less than 0.05%.

... Not available

[a]Excludes persons of Hispanic or Latino origin, unless specified.

[b]Includes public order offenses.

Source: Bureau of Justice Statistics, Annual Parole Survey, 2005, 2014, and 2015.

Estimates from the Bureau of Justice Statistics show that, at the end of 2015, 13% of all those under parole supervision were women offenders. In total, white offenders represented 44% of the U.S. parolees. In addition, 94% had more than 1-year sentence and 32% were serving a sentence for a violent crime. Instead, 8% were serving a sex crime sentence. Finally, 31% of all parolees were on parole for a drug offense (Kaeble & Bonczar, 2017).

OFFENDERS' RELEASE AND SUPERVISION

In general, the release of an offender presents many challenges. Early release can only be granted to offenders who can comply with the conditions identified in their release agreement. The level of supervision assigned depends on the risk and needs determined by the correctional institution throughout the period of confinement and the changes in the level of risk over time. Correctional institutions rely on actuarial instruments for the computation of risks for each individual (Bonta, 2002).

REVOCATION OF PAROLE

Like probation, parole is a privilege and not a right and it can be revoked. However, two U.S. Supreme Court decisions rule over the revocation of parole. In 1972, in *Morrissey v. Brewer*, the court decided that a formal hearing must be held to discuss the violations of parole prior to revocation. Later, in 1973, with *Gagnon v. Scarpelli*, the court ruled that once parole is granted, the revocation of parole must follow due process.

EX-OFFENDER EMPLOYMENT AND CRIMINAL HISTORY RECORDS

In the 1970s, scientists discussed the "moral panic" effect that increasing rates of incarceration would have on society (Cohen, 2011). The labor market is not immune to the moral panic and research evidence suggests that there is anxiety over the inclusion of ex-offenders. A criminal sentence is often the primary reason why some individuals are stigmatized (Baur, Hall, Daniels, Buckley, & Anderson, 2017). Perhaps this reaction reflects society's inability to forgive those who have made mistakes, labelling ex-offenders as "untrustworthy." This is a dilemma many employers face when screening applicants. A look at the available data shows that the majority of employers in the current labor market rely on criminal background checks to make hiring decisions (Jacobs, 2015). The main reason for this emphasis on criminal history records lies on employers' fear that ex-offenders will re-offend (Lam & Harcourt, 2003). On the other hand, recidivism rates among U.S. ex-offenders tend to be quite high. Recent estimates show that as many as 43% of those incarcerated are re-arrested within one year of their release (Durose, Cooper, & Snyder, 2014). Some believe that since this fear is not irrational, employers should be permitted to ask about criminal history. One may argue that a criminal sentence should have a beginning and an end and that ex-offenders deserve to move beyond their past and given the opportunity to become productive citizens. The issue of ex-offender employment is of particular relevance in contemporary societies. Because of restrictive social control policies, large numbers of U.S citizens have criminal history records. The scientific literature provides two relevant arguments. The first in favor of open records in labor markets which would allow employers to learn more about the situation that led to an applicant's involvement with the criminal justice system. The second supporting the idea that ex-offenders should be given the opportunity to show their skills without the threat of being dismissed solely because of their past. Both arguments have merit. However, supporters of the open records' system argue that when employers lack access to complete information about applicants, they are prone to use demographics as proxy for criminal history records, *de facto* discriminating against young black men with low educational achievement or scattered employment histories (Stoll & Bushway, 2008). A movement aimed to create fair chances for ex-offenders has spread across the United States in the last 20 years. The movement, known as "ban the box," began in the state of Hawaii in the late 1990s. The idea behind the movement is that by banning the box (or question) on criminal history records from job applications would provide applicants with records with the opportunity to prove themselves before the stigma of a criminal arrest or conviction is taken into consideration (Pager, 2008). By preventing employers from inquiring about the applicant previous encounter with the criminal justice system, applicants with criminal history records would have a chance to be evaluated on the basis of their skills rather than be judged solely because of their past. With ban the box, employers can still search applicants' criminal history records but only after an employment offer is made. Employers have the right to verify that there is no conflict between the responsibilities involved in the job and the offense for which applicants have been convicted. Ban the box policies have become very popular in the last decade. By February 2018, 30 states, the District of Columbia, and 150 cities and counties had already adopted ban the box policies for public employment. Among these, 10 states, the District of Columbia, and 31 cities and counties extended ban the box to private businesses (Avery & Hernandez, 2018). The principles highlighted in the ban the box legislation continue to be supported by researchers, but the impact of these policies is yet to be measured. While ban the box policies provide evidence of a cultural shift toward equity and fairness in the job market, research is needed to assess whether restricting access to criminal history records helps ex-offenders find jobs without any negative impact on other groups not targeted by the policies. In other words, are employers discriminating against young men of color in the labor market simply because they are more likely to carry a criminal conviction than their white peers?

FELON DISENFRACHISEMENT

For many, a criminal conviction involves the termination of their voting rights. While we would like to believe that the era of mass-incarceration is over, the impact of decades of tough on crime policies will continue to diminish the participation of many ex-offenders in local and national politics. The disenfranchisement of ex-offenders in the United States is especially concerning in that it affects disproportionately African Americans in low-income communities, a group already marginalized and under-represented in most areas of government. Estimates from the Sentencing Project indicate that 6.1 million Americans are excluded from the electorate because of a felony conviction. Among them, 2.2 million are African

Do prisoners deserve the right to vote? No

Americans (Chung, 2016). Expressed in value percent, 7.7% of African Americans are currently disenfranchised compared to 1.8% non-African Americans. However, three states (Florida, Kentucky, and Virginia) show disenfranchisement rates among African Americans that are much higher than the national average. In these states, over 20% of all African American adults are currently excluded from the electorate. Chung (2016) points out that these figures appear especially concerning when we take into consideration that 45% of those disenfranchised have already completed their criminal sentence.

Voting rights for felons vary greatly across the United States. Below is a summary of the current voting rights for felons. The data come from the results of the investigation conducted by the Brennan Institute for Justice (2018).

- In 3 states, (Iowa, Florida, and Kentucky) felons are permanently disenfranchised following a conviction, unless the government approves individual rights restoration.

- In 9 states, (Alabama, Arizona, Delaware, Massachusetts, Mississippi, Nebraska, Nevada, Tennessee, and Wyoming) some felons are permanent disenfranchised depending on the crime for which they were convicted.

- In 19 states, (Alaska, Arkansas, Georgia, Idaho, Kansas, Louisiana, Minnesota, Missouri, Nebraska, New Jersey, New Mexico, North Carolina, Oklahoma, South Carolina, Texas, Virginia, Washington, West Virginia, and Wisconsin) felons voting rights are restored upon completion of a sentence, including prison, parole, and probation.

- In 10 states, (Hawaii, Illinois, Indiana, Maryland, Massachusetts, Michigan, Montana, New Hampshire, North Dakota, and New York) voting rights are restored automatically after release from prison.
- In 2 states, (Maine and Vermont) there is no disenfranchisement for citizens with criminal records.

Following the changes in voting rights' reforms across the United States can be eye opening. While many states are moving toward more inclusive policies, some continue to exclude felons even after they complete criminal sentences. As Uggen and Manza point out, many often forget that "felons are themselves citizens, who occupy roles as taxpayers, homeowners, volunteers, and voters" (2005: 67). To accept the exclusion of groups of citizens from active participation in local and national governments might also mean to accept the idea of a crippled democracy.

LEARNING EXERCISES

Working with other students as a group divide the map of the United States in separate regions as it seems appropriate and explore the different laws and reforms that protect convicted felons. What type of patterns can you observe? What type of changes would you suggest? Prepare a handout for group discussion.

BIBLIOGRAPHY

Avery, B., & Hernandez, P. (2018). Ban the box: US cities, counties, and states adopt fair hiring policies. National Employment Law Project.

Baur, J. E., Hall, A. V., Daniels, S. R., Buckley, M. R., & Anderson, H. J. (2017). Beyond banning the box: A conceptual model of the stigmatization of ex-offenders in the workplace. *Human Resource Management Review*, *28*(2), 204–219.

Becker, H. S. (2008). *Outsiders*. New York, NY: Simon and Schuster.

Bonta, J. (2002). Offender risk assessment: Guidelines for selection and use. *Criminal Justice and Behavior*, *29*(4), 355–379.

Brennan Center for Justice (2018). Criminal disenfranchisement laws across the United States. New York University School of Law. Available at: https://www.brennancenter.org/criminal-disenfranchisement-laws-across-united-states [last visited June 11, 2018].

Chung, J. (2016). *Felony disenfranchisement: A primer*. Washington, DC: The Sentencing Project.

Clear, T. R., Reisig, M. D., & Cole, G. F. (2018). *American corrections*. Boston, MA: Cengage Learning.

Cohen, S. (2011). *Folk devils and moral panics*. London: McGibbon & Kee.

Durose, M. R., Cooper, A. D., & Snyder, H. N. (2014). *Recidivism of prisoners released in 30 states in 2005: Patterns from 2005 to 2010*. Washington, DC: US Department of Justice, Office of Justice Programs, Bureau of Justice Statistics.

Goffman, E. (1968). *Stigma: Notes on the management of spoiled identity*. Harmondsworth: Penguin.

Jacobs, J. B. (2015). *The eternal criminal record*. Harvard University Press.

Kaeble, D., & Bonczar, T. P. (2017). Probation and parole in the United States, 2015 (NCJ 250230). Washington, DC: Department of Justice.

Kaeble, D., & Glaze, L. (2017). Correctional populations in the United States, 2015. US Department of Justice Office of Justice Programs Bureau of Justice Statistics; December 2016.

Lam, H., & Harcourt, M. (2003). The use of criminal record in employment decisions: The rights of ex-offenders, employers and the public. *Journal of Business Ethics*, *47*(3), 237–252.

La Vigne, N., Davies, E., Palmer, T., & Halberstadt, R. (2008). *Release planning for successful reentry a guide for corrections, service providers, and community groups*. Washington DC: The Urban Institute

Martinson, R. (1974). What works? Questions and answers about prison reform. *The Public Interest*, (35), 22.

Mays, G. L., & Winfree Jr, L. T. (2014). *Essentials of corrections.* , Malden, MA: Wiley Blackwell.

Pager, D. (2008). *Marked: Race, crime, and finding work in an era of mass incarceration*. Chicago, IL: University of Chicago Press.

Petersilia, J. (2003). *When prisoners come home: Parole and prisoner reentry*. New York, NY: Oxford University Press.

Stoll, M. A., & Bushway, S. D. (2008). The effect of criminal background checks on hiring ex-offenders. *Criminology & Public Policy*, *7*(3), 371–404.

Travis, J. (2002). *Invisible punishment: An instrument of social exclusion.*

Travis, J. (2005). *But they all come back: Facing the challenges of prisoner reentry*. The Urban Institute.

Uggen, C., & Manza, J. (2005). Disenfranchisement and the civic reintegration of convicted felons. In C. Mele, & T. A. Miller (Eds.), *Civil Penalties: Social Consequences* (pp. 67–84). New York, NY: Routledge.

Welch, M. (2013). *Corrections: A critical approach*. New York, NY: Routledge.

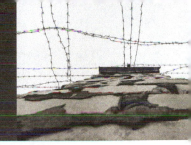

Sex Offenders on Parole:
The Case of Phillip Garrido

On the morning of June 10, 1991, 11 year old Jaycee Lee Dugard was kidnapped while waiting for the school bus in front of her family home in Lake Tahoe. Phillip Garrido and his wife Nancy shot Dugard with a stun gun before taking her away. They drove for 150 miles to return to their home in San Francisco. Once home, they hid Dugard in a shed behind their residence where they kept her for 18 years until she was freed by authorities. This was not Garrido's first offense.

In 1976, Garrido had abducted and raped a 25 years old woman. For this crime, Garrido was sentenced to 50 years in a federal prison and an additional 5 years in prison for sexual assault state charges. While incarcerated, Garrido became a model inmate and was released on parole only after 11 years. It is clear that Garrido was well behaved while in prison, but he certainly was not rehabilitated. Does complying with prison rules during incarceration provide evidence of rehabilitation? While the story of Duggard's kidnapping seems unique, offenders like Garrido exist. What can the Criminal Justice System do to protect society from people like Garrido?

During the 18 years in captivity, Dugard gave birth to two daughters fathered by Garrido. Meanwhile, parole officers made at least 60 visits at the Garridos' home. Data collected from the electronic monitoring devise showed that Garrido spent much of his time in the shed behind his residence; however, the parole officers never checked what was there. They wrote positive reports mentioning that his relationship with his wife Nancy "[was] growing and changing in a healthy manner and remaining supportive and strong" (ABC News, 2011).

Nancy's role in Phillip Garrido's crimes have left many in disbelief. She was his servant, his pimp, his accomplice. Videotapes were made public after it was revealed that Nancy would film young girls while they played on public playgrounds. Sometimes, Nancy would approach kids and ask them to perform while secretly filming them to support her husband's perversions.

The parole supervision in Garrido's case appeared to be at fault in many ways. Throughout the time Garrido was on parole, his supervisors failed to address several of his violations of parole conditions. Records indicated that several times Garrido had tested positive for using methamphetamines. Once he was even caught watering down his urine during a urine test. In 1993, he landed back to federal prison for failing a drug test. There he stayed for a whole month while his wife Nancy became Jaycee Dugard's only jailer (ABC News, 2011). Why were parole officers so lenient in Garrido's case? Was this the consequence of their heavy workload? How did Garrido play the system?

On the morning of August 24, 2009, Garrido visited the University of California with Dugard's daughters. The visit was meant to establish a collaboration that would allow him to hold a religious event. After running a criminal background check, the campus police found out that Garrido was a registered sex offender on parole. Garrido's parole supervisors were immediately contacted and suspicions grew at the news that Garrido, a known childless parolee, showed up for a meeting with two girls. A parole visitation was scheduled only two days later during which Garrido was arrested with his wife Nancy. The two admitted to the kidnapping and sexual assault of a minor. Phillip Garrido was sentenced to 413 years in prison and his wife Nancy was sentenced to 36 years in prison (ABC News, 2011).

Where does the Sex Offender Registry come from?

In 1994, the Jacob Wetterling Act mandated that every sex offender registered in the National Sex Offender Registry according to the guidelines provided by their state statute. Because of the complex patchwork of rules, a new legislative piece passed in 2006 to provide uniformity in the discipline of sex offenders, the Sex Offender Registration and Notification Act ("SORNA" or "the Act"), which is title I of the Adam Walsh Child Protection and Safety Act of 2006 (P.L. 109–248). The guidelines apply to all 50 states, the District of Columbia, the principal U.S. territories, and Indian tribal governments (U.S. Department of Justice, n.d.).

BIBLIOGRAPHY

ABC News (2011). Nightline: Crime and Punishment Series, Terry Moran reporter. Available online https://www.youtube.com/watch?v=3cK5XVeenp4 [last accessed April 23, 2018].

U.S. Department of Justice. (n.d.). Sex Offender Registration and Notification Act (SORNA). Available online https://www.justice.gov/criminal-ceos/sex-offender-registration-and-notification-act-sorna [last accessed April 23, 2018].

CPSIA information can be obtained
at www.ICGtesting.com
Printed in the USA
LVHW05s1026160818
586592LV00001B/1/P